Early Ripening

Marge Piercy is the author of ten volumes of poetry: *Breaking Camp*; *Hard Loving*; *4-Telling*; *To Be of Use*; *Living in the Open*; *The Twelve-Spoked Wheel Flashing*; *The Moon is Always Female*; *Circles on the Water*; *Stone, Paper, Knife*; and, most recently, *My Mother's Body*. She has also published nine novels: *Going Down Fast*; *Dance the Eagle to Sleep*; *Small Changes*; *Woman on the Edge of Time*; *The High Cost of Living*; *Vida*; *Braided Lives*; *Fly Away Home*; and, this year, *Gone To Soldiers*. The University of Michigan's Arbor Press published a volume of her essays, reviews and interviews as part of their Poets on Poetry series, entitled *Parti-Colored Blocks for a Quilt*. Marge Piercy has also co-authored a play, *The Last White Class*, with Ira Wood. She lives in Wellfleet, Massachusetts with Ira Wood. Her work has been translated into twelve languages. *Stone, Paper, Knife* (1983) and *My Mother's Body* (1985) are also published by Pandora Press.

PANDORA

Early Ripening

AMERICAN WOMEN'S POETRY NOW

Edited and introduced by
Marge Piercy

PANDORA

New York and London

This collection first published in the USA by
Pandora Press
(Routledge & Kegan Paul Inc.)
29 West 35th Street, New York, NY 10001
and in the UK by
Pandora Press
(Routledge & Kegan Paul Ltd)
11 New Fetter Lane
London EC4P 4EE

Set in Bembo 10/11pt.
by Columns of Reading
and printed in Great Britain
by Richard Clay Ltd
Bungay, Suffolk

Library of Congress Cataloging in Publication Data
Early ripening.
   1. American poetry—Women authors.   2. American
poetry—20th century.   I. Piercy, Marge.
PS589.E23   1987   811'.54'0809287   87–6047

British Library CIP Data also available
ISBN 0-86358-108-0(c)
      0-86358-141-2(p)

To the memory and living work
of Muriel Rukeyser
a great poet and a great example

Contents

Acknowledgments

The author and publishers would like to thank the following for permission to reproduce the poems listed below.

Katharyn Machan Aal: "Ithaca" reprinted from *The Farmers' Market Calendar 1985* (Ithaca, New York). "The Beets Poem" reprinted from *The Wings, the Vines: Poems by Katharyn Machan Aal, Alice Fulton, Karen Marie Christa Minns, and Sybil Smith*, published by McBooks Press (1983). Reprinted by permission of the author.

Ai: "The Prisoner" reprinted from *Sin* published by Houghton Mifflin, copyright © 1986 by Ai. Reprinted by permission of Houghton Mifflin Company.

Ellen Bass: "Live for it" reprinted from *Woman of Power*. "To praise" reprinted from *Calyx* and "Change", reprinted by permission of the author.

Beth Brant: "Ride the Turtle's Back" and excerpt reprinted from "A Simple Act" reprinted from *Mohawk Trail*. Reprinted by permission of the author.

Barbara Brinson Curiel: "Pearl," "Recipe for Sand" and "Recipe for Salt" reprinted by permission of the author.

Mary Pierce Brosmer: "Mothers: A Meditation" and "Limited Access" reprinted by permission of the author.

Lorna Dee Cervantes: "Visions of Mexico While at a Writing Symposium in Port Townsend, Washington" and "Beneath the Shadow of the Freeway" reprinted from *Emplumada* by Lorna Dee Cervantes by permission of the University of Pittsburgh Press. Copyright © 1981 by Lorna Dee Cervantes.

Amy Clampitt: "Venice Revisited" and "George Eliot Country". Reprinted by permission; copyright © 1984 Amy Clampitt. Originally in the *New Yorker*.

Michelle Cliff: "The Land of Look Behind" and "I-tie-all-my-people-together" reprinted by permission of the author.

Lucille Clifton: "poem," "winnie song" and "album" reprinted by permission of the author.

Jane Cooper: "Rent," "Jittoku, Buddhist Mystic – 15th Century," and "Conversation by the Body's Light" from

Song of Bullets" reprinted from *Dangerous Music* (San Francisco: Momo's Press), by permission of the author.

Joy Harjo: "Bleed Through," "Nine Below" and "Resurrection" reprinted from *Tyuonyi* (Santa Fe, New Mexico: Institute of American Indian Arts Press), and "Mercy" reprinted by permission of the author. "She Had Some Horses" and "The Woman Hanging from the Thirteenth Floor Window" reprinted by permission of Thunder's Mouth Press and the author.

Linda Hogan: "The Other Side," "To Light" and "Seeing Through the Sun" reprinted from *Seeing Through the Sun* (University of Massachusetts Press) and "The New Apartment, Minneapolis" reprinted by permission of the author.

June Jordan: "Getting Down to Get Over" reprinted by permission of the author.

Faye Kicknosway: "Lament:", "Gracie, 1967" and excerpt from "Night Braid" reprinted by permission of the author and publishers.

Carolyn Kizer: "The Intruder," "A Widow in Wintertime" and "Thrall" reprinted by permission of the author.

Irena Klepfisz: Dedication from "Bashert" and "Royal Pearl" reprinted from *Keeper of Accounts* (Sinister Wisdom Books) and *Different Enclosures: Poetry and Prose of Irena Klepfisz* (Onlywomen Press). "Etlekhe verter oyf mame-loshn/A few words in the mother tongue" reprinted from *The Tribe of Dina: A Jewish Women's Anthology* (Sinister Wisdom Books). All reprinted by permission of the author.

Maxine Kumin: "Our Ground Time Here Will Be Brief," "Relearning the Language of April," "Changing the Children" and "Making the Jam Without You" all reprinted from *Our Ground Time Here Will Be Brief* by Maxine Kumin. © 1976, 1977, 1978, 1979, 1980 by Maxine Kumin. "Shopping in Ferney with Voltaire" and "Grandchild" from *The Long Approach* by Maxine Kumin. Copyright © 1982, 1984 by Maxine Kumin. Reprinted by permission of Viking Penguin and the author.

Meridel LeSueur: "I Light Your Streets," "Shelter Him in Milk and Meadow" and "Rites of Ancient Ripening" reprinted by permission of the author.

Denise Levertov: "Making Peace," "The Mockingbird of Mockingbirds", "The Absentee" and "Zeroing In" from Denise Levertov, *Breathing the Water*. Copyright © 1987 by Denise Levertov. Reprinted by permission of New Directions Publishing Corporation.

Lyn Lifshin: "Afterward," "The No More Apologizing the No More Little Laughing Blues," "My Mother and the Bed," "Plymouth Women" and "Thirty Miles West of Chicago" all reprinted by permission of the author.

Audre Lorde: "Chain," "Hanging Fire" and "The Women of

Bee Bee Tan: "Pontianak" and "Curfew" reprinted by permission of the author.

Susan Tichy: "Orpheus" first published in *Beloit Poetry Journal.* "Orpheus" and "The Cry That Kills the Senses" reprinted by permission of the author.

Kitty Tsui: "Don"t Call Me Sir Call Me Strong," excerpt from "Red Rock Canyon, Summer 1977" "the vision" and "chinatown talking story" reprinted by permission of the author.

Mona Van Duyn: "Letters From a Father" from *Letters from a Father and Other Poems.* Copyright © 1982 Mona Van Duyn. Reprinted with the permission of Atheneum Publishers, Inc.

Lisa Vice: "Houston Street," "To the Waitress at the Hickory Pit" and "Cambodia Witness" reprinted by permission of the author.

Diane Wakoski: "I Have Had to Learn to Live with My Face" and "Coda: Greed Part 12—Looking for Beethoven in Las Vegas" reprinted by permission of the author.

Marilyn Nelson Waniek: "Mama's Promises" and "Dinosaur Spring". Reprinted by permission of Louisiana State University Press from *Mama's Promise* by Marilyn Nelson Waniek. © 1985.

Roberta Hill Whiteman: "Acknowledgement," "Fogbound" and "In Mosa's Time" reprinted by permission of the author.

Nellie Wong: "Have Head, Have Tail" and "Eat, Eat!" reprinted by permission of the author.

Evan Zimroth: "Separations," "Planting Children: 1939" and "Front Porch: A Drama Critic Warns of Clichés" reprinted by permission of the author.

Introduction

Putting together an anthology reminded me of organizing an enormous dinner party where one quarter of the guests are strict vegans, one quarter demand to be served rare beef, one quarter are allergic to wheat or fruit or milk products and the remaining quarter are on macrobiotic yoga low phlegm sufi diets—while depending on pot luck to provide the food. Nobody is bound to be entirely pleased by the choices, but you hope it comes together somewhere, if only in the mind of the Ideal Eater.

Several observations forced themselves on me as I edited. Women's poetry of our time is at its best characterized by an absence of the disassociation of sensibility T. S. Eliot wrote about. Contemporary women's poetry tends to be, far more seamlessly than contemporary men's poetry, of the body, the brain, the emotions fused. It is not as commonly poetry of alienation (although there are women poets in this volume who are striking exceptions to all these and all other general remarks I make, since I have sought out a diversity of language, style, approach, form and themes).

At the same time, *vis-à-vis* almost any institution or holiday or habit or idea, there is a confrontational aspect, a remaking, a renewing, a renaming, a re-experiencing and then recasting. We have a problematic relationship to almost any aspect of the society or culture received or inflicted upon us. Some poets see themselves vectored by various oppressions and identities and may sometimes wonder, as Audre Lorde asked in a poem not in this collection:

> which me will survive
> all these liberations
> "Who Said It Was Simple,"
> **Chosen Poems**

Another aspect that struck me was that a number of us are engaged in the quest for female godhead, the recreation or creation from scratch, from history and dream and vision, of a mythology and a cosmology that lead to us, instead of excluding us or sticking us in as an afterthought. We have a genuine god or goddess hunger that is creating icons, lives and words of the prophets and saints, visions and prescriptions for visions. There is also a rootedness in earth, in the powers of land and the connection with other living creatures that is in its origins Native American, characteristic of several of those poets included, but also part of the vision of other women poets. The essential vision

1

of feminism rests on that sense of the self not apart from nature, not above, not instrumental, but on an awareness of being part of the whole, which is holy.

A number of the themes are those I expected before I began, the continuity and sense of inheritance and of betrayal from generation to generation, grandmother to mother to daughter to her daughter and on. Poems about birthing and mothering are new, because mostly women who had children could not be poets, previously, could not create for us out of their lives.

As I hope this anthology demonstrates, women are writing immensely exciting, approachable, rich, funny and moving poetry that can speak to a wider readership than it usually gets. Women are writing much of the best poetry being written, way more than half of it I believe, but remain poorly represented in anthologies, textbooks, reading series, prize lists, awards and every other institution controlled by white men who like the way things are presently run just fine. Women are still mostly read by women; men remain under the delusion that the poetry women write will not speak to them. I think that means that many men miss out on poetry that could get them far more involved than what they're inclined to read, or more likely, inclined to bow the head at and pass by: that's high culture, may it rest in peace.

Aesthetics is written after the fact, like laws passed after a coup, and history changes because the outcome is different. I agreed with my publisher that it is appropriate now to put together a women's anthology of American poetry. The wave of anthologies of the early 1970s brought many new poets to readers, but some of those poets have slipped out of poetry since, others are in mid-career, new ones have come along and women poets have created a large body of contemporary work that I think must change the assessment and finally the shape of all of the writing of our era. It is really about time to do an anthology of poetry that includes male poets in that same landscape and looks at them in the perspective of the exciting work that women are producing. However, failing that, we should look at the women's landscape and realize how densely populated and beautifully planted it is, with designs beginning to emerge as the trees come of age, and bear cones and fruit and make good hard wood.

This then is not promise but delivery, not so much a women's culture as a contribution to a culture that must now be for and of women's experiences as well as men's, that must change to accommodate such rich, diverse and powerful work. We are past the point where critics, whether reviewing a few poetry books in the London *Times* or *New York Times*, or for literary magazines, editors, teachers of literature and male poets themselves can pontificate about poetry and mean only the work of twenty or thirty white male writers.

One aspect of this anthology which impressed itself on me before I was through was that it ought to be twice as long. There are many poets who ought to be in here and aren't because I had filled the space permitted me before I ran across their work, or because of delays in reaching them, letters returned from old addresses, gone astray, eaten by mad machines in the mysterious bowels of the automated and ever slower Post Office. There are six poets I found in between completing the collection and writing this Introduction who should have been included. Inevitably I started with poets whose work was familiar to me, who have sent me books, and whose work I have regularly seen, and then I moved out from there.

This is not a collection of my friends, and indeed, may make some of my friends angry. I did not include some people whose work I have admired and praised, because I felt recent work was less exciting than that of poets I do not know personally, or because I feel poetry has ceased to be a central passion for them. Only one poet I approached refused to be in a women's anthology. Although a few others expressed skittishness or reservations, they gave me good poems. The vast majority of my correspondents were pleased I had taken on a task that they and I judged essential if finally thankless. But not joyless.

I had a recurring fantasy of collecting the poems in person. I found it a great pleasure when I could attach faces and personalities and bodies to Colleen McElroy and Joy Harjo; I wish I could meet every one of the women in here. I imagined hearing each of their voices in my ears as well as my head.

It was also impossible not to notice that racism takes a real toll in the arts, that a high proportion of the women of color I was corresponding with had just had a death of someone very close to them, had a serious debilitating or life-threatening disease, had financial problems that were causing them to take jobs unrelated to their work, had recently had to move four times and couldn't get their mail, or had just disappeared, just plain disappeared. Life is not a bed of cushy jobs and fat grants for any but a couple of poets in this book, but still the discrepancy was striking.

What have I looked for? It is my sense that the first ripening is with us and that we can see something of the work women have enabled each other to do, the dead preparing for us as indeed the living still open for us new rooms, new roads out and in, discovering new comets and breeding new flowers.

I have looked for intensity, richness of connection, strength, lyric voice. It has been hard to limit the poets and hard to choose a meager handful of poems from their full and amazing range. It is my conviction that currently in the United States, more women than men are writing good and vital poetry, although there are fine male poets. This is our renaissance, our Elizabethan plenty. We have giants like Adrienne Rich, Audre Lorde, Diane di Prima and Maxine Kumin, we have rising powers like Joy Harjo and Celia Gilbert and Sharon Olds, and we have dozens and dozens of individual voices sharply flavored and yet of our time, our flesh, our troubles.

I had not imagined how much work this anthology would be, which is just as well. I suspect that anthologizing is addictive, anyhow. It is much like picking flowers in early summer, when there are more than you can possibly bring in, because flowers are beautiful and these poets have done wonderful work, and it doesn't matter how you cram them in the vase, it is hard to create an ugly bouquet.

The work represented here is multi-cultural, because women's work is, and women of color are strongly represented, as they must be in any honest survey of contemporary poetry. Because women of color have even more trouble getting published than white women do, and are often left out of surveys, anthologies, reading series, I am sure that I have missed work by many such women who rightfully should have been included, but I tried hard to find them.

For work to be written, it must first be conceived. The work of women in naming our experiences enables each of us to hold on to what has happened to us, to insights we had at fifteen and lost because we lacked a framework of ideas we could use to interpret our adventures and misadventures of the mind and body. Every woman who begins to create artifacts that deliver to us news and energy from her experience empowers more of us to create from ours. We rebound and surge forward from each other's work. Our imaginations are freed from constraints we only become aware of as they vanish.

For work to be published and stay in print, there must be an audience demanding something like it, even if it never existed until that moment: women insisting on reading about women, insisting on understanding ourselves, in sharing insight and speculation, in seeing our small daily fusses and our larger agonies and achievements used with respect to make art, create a public space in which such art may stand. Critics come along and erect a protective barrier of explanation, explication, justification that prevents immediate demolition.

Even to conceive of new work, we must fight inner demons that censor and choke, that bid us be fey, to conceal our meaning, to play it safe. Ten years ago there was a warmth between women poets that is often lacking today. That's a pity. That warmth was based on understanding that we were workers in a common endeavor. Often now younger women will act as if they truly believe that the simple existence of older women of accomplishment in some way diminishes them, leading to snide attacks, as if to hack away at other writers' work gave them more space, more attention. That is nonsense and comes from bad Hemingway analogies between sports and writing. We don't have champions or simple hierarchies. In truth, if someone writes a good work in some genre, readers are more apt to seek out that genre. Good work in a field breeds interest and makes room for more good practitioners. We are not rivals but workers building something whose final shape we are not able even to fantasize.

Those of us who began to create a consciously female poetry and those of us who began to create a consciously feminist poetry are the target for male and female critics who resent us and review our work in terms of politics they disagree with, or who simply ignore our accomplishments. As for younger writers, instead of replicating the old war of mothers and daughters, let us go along together in many directions at once, understanding that even as we are part of all living creatures in a seamless web of life sharing the same earth, the same chemicals and the same energy, simmering in the same soup of time, we are all part of poetry and we make of and for each other as well as ourselves. We are still all enabling and empowering each other.

I think if I could back off enough, perhaps almost to Venus, this anthology would have a shape that would astonish and enlighten me, but I am only the collector. Enjoy this cornucopia. Some of it will please you, some of it may annoy, but I hope little will bore you. These are our first fruits.

One word I must explain is "American" in the title: there is simply no other convenient adjective for citizens of the United States, however aggrandizing such use may be.

Katharyn Machan Aal

Ithaca

Today at the Farmer's Market
goat cheese, tiny tart grapes,
a catnip toy, one loaf of George's
whole wheat bread, two baskets
of Red Havens picked this morning
seven miles away. The good life:

that's what we say, all those
who work for not enough money
in order to stay in this town
where bookstores beckon on a dozen streets
and three hills curve up green and steep
above the swan-necked lake.

The Iroquois Nation knew this land
as holy spirit place, told stories
that have sunk into the weeds.
Now we who call it our home
summon spirits with different names:
ease, struggle, love. Living

here along the edges of gorges
we give our reasons, smile,
minds knowing only half of why
our breath needs this gray sky.

The Beets Poem

Beets: now there's a subject.
Dark red, rounded, hard as—
well, hard as beets.

I know a woman
who grew a garden last summer,
planted it with nothing
but lettuce and beets.
The lettuce didn't grow
but she had plenty of slugs

and beets, plenty of beets.
Now whenever anyone visits her
she takes them down cellar,
says, "See my beets?"
And there they are, pickled,
row after row of dark red jars
no one will ever open.

Someone else I know
always asks for beets, no matter
what kind of restaurant we're in.
Even at the beach
he'll go up to the hot dog stand.
"Got any beets?" he'll say.
And when the man at the grill
just stares at him, he sighs
and turns away, and spends
half an hour just gazing at the waves.

I know what you're thinking.
Why don't I introduce these friends,
have them both to dinner
one night, serve vegetarian?
It's not so easy.
Remember, beets is our subject,
and beets is what I hate about them both.

Ai

The Prisoner

1

Yesterday, the man who calls himself "Our Father"
made me crawl on smashed Coke bottles.
Today, I sleep. I think I sleep,
till someone beats on the door, with what?—
sticks, pans—but I don't move.
I'm used to it.
Still, when Our Father rushes into the room
and drags me out, I feel the old fear.
In the interrogation room,
he knocks me to the floor,
then sits on the side of his desk,
his arms folded, that sad look on his face
I know so well. He shakes his head slowly,
stops, and smiles.
"I've got something special today," he says,
"for a fucking whore of a terrorist bitch."
I want to say nothing,
knowing how denial angers him,
but I can't stop myself.
I'm not a terrorist, I say.
"That's not what I heard," he replies, standing up.
"Aren't you the friend of a friend of a friend
of a terrorist son of a bitch
who was heard two years ago to say
that someone ought to do something
about this government?"
I don't answer.
Already, I've begun to admit that it must be true.
"I lack just one thing," he says, "the name."
"I know you think you're innocent,
but you aren't.
Everyone is guilty."
He slaps me, then pushes one side of my face
toward the green glass.

2

I've been stung by a swarm of bees.
I'm eight. I'm running for the pond
on my uncle Oscar's farm.
Oscar, I cry. Our Father sighs deeply,

8

lifts me up, and sets me down in a chair.
"This Oscar," he says, handing me a notebook and pen,
"where can I find him?"
I don't hesitate, as I take the pen
and set it down
on the clean, blank paper.

3
Our Father lets me off
a block from my apartment.
He keeps the motor running,
but comes and leans
against the car beside me.
I try to guess the month. March, April? I say.
He tells me it's September,
to just take a look at the sky.
Then he tells me he was a prisoner once too.
I stare at his face,
the dry, sallow skin,
the long scar running from temple to chin.
"Oh this," he touches the scar gently,
"I got this playing soccer.
No, the real scars don't show.
You should know that.
You need time, though, to sort it all out.
I'm still a young man,
but sometimes I feel as old as the Bible.
But this is a celebration."
He takes a bottle of wine from the car
and we drink, while the stars glitter above us.
Done, he tosses the bottle into the street.
"Freedom," he says, "freedom is something you earn.
The others don't understand that, but we do."

Ellen Bass

Live for it

Window curtain nodding in the May breeze
birds outside singing their high sweet scatter
inside a fly frantic against its mistake, buzzing the walls, the
                                                            glass,
        small thuds of failure—

Since my daughter's birth five rich years ago, I have never been
                                                            without
        the mantle of nuclear holocaust.
I feel it like crepe against my cheek.

The first year, I wept.
The exhaustion of nighttime nursing,
the demand of infant need,
the tidal love that broke upon my abundant body
        left me sensible to knowledge I had shielded from so deftly
                                                            before.

She reads now, prints, bounces a ball, ties bows,
        washes her feet in the bath.
She says, "If you read one more story,
        I'll let you sleep as late as you want in the morning."
She says, "Let's make up. We don't want to fight."
She says, "I love you more than I love you,"
        which means, according to Snoopy she explains, "No
                                                            bombs."

Nights, I watch her sleep, the glow of new being rosy on her skin
her breath, strawberries in the sun.
She is healthy, bright, funny.
If we lived in other times, I would say, "Kineahora, let her be
                                                            well,"
        as my mother before me, hers before her.
And I would take care not to brag, protecting my naches from the
                                                            wrath
        of God or neighbors.
Yet inside I'd be smug. Contentment would tingle my blood like
                                                            chablis.

Today I have no assurance,
only fear, fierce hope, and these precious days.
I no longer forget what is precious.

The curtain still bobs, the birds trill
the fly has chanced through the open window
and is on with its life—
maybe chances is inaccurate.
It worked, tried over and over, hurling itself against all surfaces
                                                            until
        one did not resist and it was met by the familiar currents
                                                        of wind

Can that happen to us?
Miracles happen. What is nature but the most complex, amazing
                                                        miracle?
Jasmine unfolding, the scent and color attracting the bees,
        the darker veins guiding them toward the nectar,
honey in honeycombs, worms aerating soil, the levity of bird
                                                        bones,
        fins of fish, the eye blinking—
who could have ever conceived it?
the crescent moon, tender as new love in the luminescent blue,
milkweed silk—who could have imagined it?

And my lover, when she lifts her lips to me and I first feel that
                                                        softness
        warm like summer nights as a child
when she rubs against me like fur
and small cries escape my mouth like birds,
"Sing to me," she breathes
and I sing glory I did not know was mine to sing.

What is this but a miracle?
What is this but the improbable, marvelous reward of desire?

Desire—that fire I was taught to suspect,
        that intensity I struggled to calm.
"Don't want too much," the voices warned.

No.   Want.   Want life.
Want this fragile oasis of the galaxy to flourish.
Want fertility, want seasons, want this spectacular array of
                                                        creatures,
this brilliant balance of need.

Want it. Want it all.
Desire. Welcome her raging power.
May her strength course through us.
Desire, she is life. Desire life.
Allow ourselves to desire life, to want this sweetness
so passionately, that we live for it.

Change

This is where I yank the old roots
from my chest, like the tomatoes
we let grow until December, stalks
thick as saplings.

This is the moment when the ancient fears
race like thoroughbreds, asking for more
and more rein. And I, the driver,
for some reason they know nothing of
strain to hold them back.

Terror grips me like a virus
and I sweat, fevered,
trying to burn it out.

This feat is so invisible. All you can see
is a woman going about her ordinary day,
drinking tea, taking herself to the movies,
reading in bed. If victorious
I will look exactly the same.

Yet I am hoisting a car from mud ruts
half a century deep. I am hacking
a clearing through the fallen slash
of my heart. Without laser precision,
with only the primitive knife of need, I cut
and splice the circuitry of my brain.
I change.

To praise

I want to praise bodies
nerves and synapses
the impulse that travels the spine
        like fish darting

I want to praise the mouth
that warm wet lair where the tongue reclines
and the tongue, roused
        slithering a cool path

I want to praise hands
those architects that create us anew
fingers, cartographers, revealing
        who we can become
and palms, cupped priestesses
        worshipping the long slow curve

I want to praise muscle
and the heart, that flamboyant champion
        with its insistent pelting like
        tropical rain

Hair, the sweep of it
        a breeze

and feet, arch taut
        stretching like cats

I want to praise the face, engraved
like a river bed; it breaks like morning
        like a piñata, festival of hope

Breasts, cornucopia
nipples that jump up, gleeful
        like a child greeting the day

and clitoris, shimmering
a huge tender pearl
        in that succulent oyster

I want to praise the love cries
sharp, brilliant as ice
and the roar that swells in the lungs
        like an avalanche

I want to praise the gush, the hot
spring thaw of it, the rivers
        wild with it

Bodies, our extravagant bodies

And I want to praise you, how you have
lavished yours
upon mine
        until I want to praise

Beth Brant

Ride the Turtle's Back

A woman grows hard and skinny.
She squeezes into small corners.
Her quick eyes uncover dust and cobwebs.
She reaches out
for flint and sparks fly in the air.
Flames turned loose on fields
burn down to bare seeds
we planted deep.

The corn is white and sweet.
Under its pale, perfect kernels
a rotting cob is betrayal.
It lies in our bloated stomachs.

I lie in Grandmother's bed
and dream the earth into a turtle.
She carries us slowly across the universe.
The sun warms us.
At night the stars do tricks.
The moon caresses us.

We are listening for the sounds of food.
Mother is giving birth, Grandmother says.
Corn whispers.
The earth groans with labor
turning corn yellow in the sun.

I lie in Grandmother's bed.

We listen.

from A Simple Act (Story Two: My House)

I write because to not write is a breach of faith.

Out of a past where amnesia was the expected.
Out of a past occupied with quiet.
Out of a past, I make truth for a future.

Cultures gone up in flames.
The smell of burning leather, paper, flesh, filling the
spaces where memory fails.
The smell of a chestnut tree, its leaves making magic.
The smell of Sandra's hair, like dark coffee and incense.

I close my eyes. Pictures unreeling on my eyelids.
Portraits of beloved people flashing by quickly.
Opening my eyes, I think of the seemingly ordinary
things that women do. And how, with the brush of an
eyelash against a cheek, the movement of pen on paper,
power is born.

A gourd is a hollowed-out shell, used as a utensil.

We make our bowls from the stuff of nature. Of life.

We carve and scoop, discarding the pulp.

Ink on paper, picking up trails I left so many lives ago.

Leaving my mark, my footprints, my sign.

I write what I know.

Barbara Brinson Curiel

Pearl

You left
the taste
of your flesh,
a pearl,
growing
in my mouth.

Recipe for Sand

One ocean
    cupped in stone
    magnetized grope
    toward tantalizing heavens.

Crusts of shore
    simple in their ache
    for the foamy caress
    of water.

Teal Blue
    boiled out
    by the friction of
    of harmony.

Seaweed
    to bind
    this convulsion
    together.

One moon, one sun.

Fish bone

Seashell

Fossil

Salt.

Recipe for Salt

Fuzz on the lip of seashells
    tuna sweating for the moon.

Mineral armor of seahorses
    tears between the fingers of stars.

Scapular embrace of crystal
    blazing saline sanctity.

White whalebone of sodium
    chloride caress.

Mary Pierce Brosmer

Mothers: A Meditation

They visit me often now,
gather in my room
nights I cannot sleep,
nights I lie in bed sifting
through house noises for the
reassuring sound of my son's
breathing,
nights I pray for sleep.

They seem to want something,
stretch white hands toward me,
want to give me, ask me,
tell me something,
and I cannot sleep.

and I hear nuns intone
the sand round tones of the Stabat Mater,
hear the click and tink of their
rosaries as they process into my room
in two swaying, candlelit lines,
their white faces rising moons
in the darkness,

Aunt Marie snaps beans into her
aproned lap, her hands are red,
knuckles swollen, nails and moons
round and white, white moons of
childhood rising, rain tapping
the old tin roof, breeze heavy
with the scent of cape jasmine
lifting the lace drapes, fanning
my hot face.

and Mother, white-gloved and smiling,
rises from the darkness of old photographs,
gardenias in her black hair, to crown
the Blessed Virgin, arms floury to the
elbows, her hair now streaked with white,
she pats fat moons of dough into dumpling
pans, lays her cool hands on
my feverish cheeks.

Suffering mothers, cool, white mothers,

I love you, will tell your lives
like beads, recite your days like decades:

the Joyful, Sorrowful, Glorious mysteries
you teach. I reach for the beads, clear
and lovely in the moonlight, touch
your hands, and finally, sleep.

Limited Access

Statistically,
this is the most
dangerous stretch
of highway,
this necessary stretch
between
loving and
letting go.

The curves so treacherously
banked,
the traffic dense,
drivers with eyes
nearly closed
in concentration.

What am I doing here?
I who love
being driven
better
than driving?

My hands on the wheel
are not the gloved
leather of those
in charge.
They are small, white,
tentative.

I drive this loop
passengerless
commuting daily
promising myself a new road
tomorrow,
a safe route
with trees and barns
for landmarks.

Then you pass me
going the opposite direction

and I press the accelerator
to the floor
bearing down
on the nearest
exit.

Lorna Dee Cervantes

Beneath the Shadow of the Freeway

1
Across the street—the freeway,
blind worm, wrapping the valley up
from Los Altos to Sal Si Puedes.
I watched it from my porch
unwinding. Every day at dusk
as Grandma watered geraniums
the shadow of the freeway lengthened.

2
We are a woman family:
Grandma, our innocent Queen;
Mama, the Swift Knight, Fearless Warrior.
Mama wanted to be Princess instead.
I know that. Even now she dreams of taffeta
and foot-high tiaras.

Myself: I could never decide.
So I turned to books, those staunch, upright men.
I became Scribe: Translator of Foreign Mail,
interpreting letters from the government, notices
of dissolved marriages and Welfare stipulations.
I paid the bills, did light man-work, fixed faucets,
insured everything
against all leaks.

3
Before rain I notice seagulls.
They walk in flocks,
cautious across lawns: splayed toes,
indecisive beaks. Grandma says
seagulls mean storm.

In California in the summer,
mockingbirds sing all night.
Grandma says they are singing for their nesting wives.
"They don't leave their families
borrachando."

She likes the ways of birds,
respects how they show themselves
for toast and a whistle.

She believes in myths and birds.
She trusts only what she builds
with her own hands.

21

4

She built her house,
cocky, disheveled carpentry,
after living twenty-five years
with a man who tried to kill her.

Grandma, from the hills of Santa Barbara,
I would open my eyes to see her stir mush
in the morning, her hair in loose braids,
tucked close around her head
with a yellow scarf.

Mama said, "It's her own fault,
getting screwed by a man for that long.
Sure as shit wasn't hard."
soft she was soft

5

in the night I would hear it
glass bottles shattering the street
words cracked into shrill screams
inside my throat   a cold fear
as it entered the house in hard
unsteady steps   stopping at my door
my name   bathrobe   slippers
outside a 3 A.M. mist heavy
as a breath full of whiskey
stop it   go home   come inside
mama if he comes here again
I'll call the police

inside
a gray kitten   a touchstone
purring beneath the quilts
grandma stitched
from his suits
the patchwork singing
of mockingbirds

6

"You're too soft . . . always were.
You'll get nothing but shit.
Baby, don't count on nobody."
—a mother's wisdom.
Soft. I haven't changed,
maybe grown more silent, cynical
on the outside.

"O Mama, with what's inside of me
I could wash that all away. I could."

"But Mama, if you're good to them
they'll be good to you back."

Back. The freeway is across the street.
It's summer now. Every night I sleep with a gentle man

to the hymn of mockingbirds,

and in time, I plant geraniums.
I tie up my hair into loose braids,
and trust only what I have built
with my own hands.

Visions of Mexico While at a Writing Symposium in Port Townsend, Washington

México
When I'm that far south, the old words
molt off my skin, the feathers
of all my nervousness.
My own words somersault naturally as my name,
joyous among all those meadows: Michoacán,
Vera Cruz, Tenochtitlán, Oaxaca. . . .
Pueblos green on the low hills
where men slap handballs below acres of maíz.
I watch and understand.
My frail body has never packed mud
or gathered in the full weight of the harvest.
Alone with the women in the adobe, I watch men,
their taut faces holding in all their youth.
This far south we are governed by the law
of the next whole meal. We work
and watch seabirds elbow their wings
in migratory ways, those mispronouncing gulls
coming south
to refuge or gameland.

I don't want to pretend I know more
and can speak all the names. I can't.
My sense of this land can only ripple through my veins
like the chant of an epic corrido.
I come from a long line of eloquent illiterates
whose history reveals what words don't say.
Our anger is our way of speaking,
the gesture is an utterance more pure than word.
We are not animals
but our senses are keen and our reflexes,
accurate punctuation.
All the knifings in a single night, low-voiced
scufflings, sirens, gunnings. . . .
We hear them
and the poet within us bays.

Washington
I don't belong this far north.
The uncomfortable birds gawk at me.

They hem and haw from their borders in the sky.
I heard them say: México is a stumbling comedy.
A loose-legged Cantinflas woman
acting with Pancho Villa drunkenness.
Last night at the tavern
this was all confirmed
in a painting of a woman: her glowing
silk skin, a halo
extending from her golden coiffure
while around her, dark-skinned men with Jap slant eyes
were drooling in a caricature of machismo.
Below it, at the bar, two Chicanas
hung at their beers. They had painted black
birds that dipped beneath their eyelids.
They were still as foam while the men
fiddled with their asses, absently;
the bubbles of their teased hair snapped
open in the forced wind of the beating fan.

there are songs in my head I could sing you
songs that could drone away
all the Mariachi bands you thought you ever heard
songs that could tell you what I know
or have learned from my people
but for that   I need words
simple black nymphs between white sheets of paper
obedient words   obligatory words   words I steal
in the dark when no one can hear me

as pain sends seabirds south from the cold
I come north
to gather my feathers
for quills

Amy Clampitt

Venice Revisited

> While the Frenchmen and Flemings abandoned themselves in a frenzy
> of wholesale destruction, the Venetians kept their heads. They knew
> beauty when they saw it.
>
> John Julius Norwich,
> *A History of Venice*

1

Guise and disguise, the mirroring and masquerades:
brocaded wallowings, ascensions, levitations:
glimmering interiors, beaked motley; the hide-
and-seek of Tintoretto and Carpaccio. From within
walled gardens' green enclave, a blackbird's warble—
gypsy non sequitur out of root-cumbered
terra firma, a mainland stepped from
to this shored-up barge, this Bucintoro
of mirage, of artifice. Outside the noon-dim
dining room, the all-these-years-uninterrupted
sloshing of canals; bagged refuse, ungathered
filth; the unfed cats, still waiting.
                     To breathe again
the faint stink of this place I had not thought to
revisit in this life; to catch, through shutters
half-latched for the siesta, the same glimpse
of a young girl's laundry—a glimpse half-
preternatural, like an encounter with some
evidence of resurrection: re-entering, to swim
above the mild tumuli of San Marco,
that last surreal upwelling of Byzantium,
is also to disinter the vertigo
of the homesteader's wife who, numb
in the face of the undisguised
prospect of the place she'd come to, drove
a post into the yard outside the sodhouse
to have something, she said, to look at.

2

The place they'd come to—treeless, its sole prospect
the watery skin-scurf of reedbeds, of mudflats
cowering shivering in the dark or sweltering
at noon, no place to hide from vertigo—was no
less desolate. They lived at first
dispersed, in dens of osier and wattle,

25

hemmed by no familiar dolomite, no tree-blurred
watershed to lift the eyes to—the lagoon
a wan presentiment of the great basin's
vastness—a place for a homesteader's wife
to drift and drown, or else to settle and
grow stolid as a driven post in.
                                    Postpiles driven
into the muck of the lagoon—a million-plus of them,
a thousand-plus times over—would one day undergird
the multiplicity of domes, arcades, facades
of variegated marble, stilts for the stupendous
masquerade of history: the Bucintoro
with the Doge afloat, rowed to the cheering
of lubricious throngs, the whimpering
of lutes: a stage set above the windings
of these onetime sloughs, the hidden
thoroughfares obscure and treacherous
as the dim wagon tracks the homesteaders
would inevitably follow into the disguiseless
grassland, the desolation of
the place they'd come to.

3

Magnificence of guise and disguise, of the given
and the taken: that a body thought to be
that of Saint Mark—Evangelist, witness to
the crime that had then given birth to faith,
subscriber to the possibility of resurrection—
had been brought here from somewhere, is
believed to be historical. Whether the box
they brought it in—the filched cadaver,
the purported-to-be sacred relic—in fact contained
merely another masquerade, has long since
ceased to matter. Maskers, lovers of shows,
of music, looters who knew beauty when
they saw it, who (while others rampaged,
raped, or merely smashed) made off with
the famous four bronze horses, and much else,
they did know beauty: give them
at least that credit.
                           What stolen relics,
sacred or bogus, what odor of sanctity
or of corruption, would the descendants
of the homesteader's wife who drove
that post to keep herself from going
mad, bring home, may yet bring home to
the likewise unhandsomely acquired
terrain she'd come to? What mainland—
if there is a mainland any more for any
émigré's descendants to return to—
can they claim? What's to be said for
their, for our own faltering empire,
our most unserene republic, other

than that while crusaders of our own
rampaged in Asia, one set foot also
on the maskless, indubitable
wasteland of the moon?

George Eliot Country
for Gordon Haight

From this Midland scene—glum slag heaps,
barge canals, gray sheep, the vivid overlap
of wheat field and mustard hillside like
out-of-season sunshine, the crabbed silhouette
of oak trees (each joint a knot, each knot
a principled demurral: tough, arthritic, stubborn
as the character of her own father—fame,
the accretion of a Pyrrhic happiness, had
exiled her to London, with its carriages
and calling cards, its screaming headaches.

Griff House—dear old Griff, she wistfully
apostrophized it—in those days still intact,
its secrets kept, has now been grated to a
motel-cum-parking lot beside the trunk road,
whose raw, ungainly seam of noise cuts through
the rainy solace of Griff Lane: birdsong,
coal smoke, the silvered powderings of
blackthorn, a flowering cherry tree's
chaste flare, the sludge-born, apoplectic
screech of jet aircraft tilting overhead.

The unmapped sources that still fed nostalgia
for a rural childhood survive the witherings
of retrospect: the look of brickyards,
stench of silk mills, scar of coal mines,
the knife of class distinction: wall-enclosed,
parkland-embosomed, green-lawned Arbury Hall,
fan vaulting's stately fakeries, the jewel-
stomachered, authentic shock of Mary Fitton and
her ilk portrayed, the view of fishponds—school
and role model of landed-proprietary England.

Born in the year of Peterloo, George Eliot
had no illusions as to the expense of such
emoluments. Good society (she wrote), floated
on gossamer wings of light irony, required no less
than an entire, arduous national existence
condensed into unfragrant, deafening factories,
cramped into mines, sweating at furnaces, or
scattered in lonely houses on the clayey or chalky

27

cornland . . . where Maggie Tulliver, despairing
of gentility, ran off to join the Gypsies.

Violets still bloom beside the square-towered
parish church where Mary Anne was christened;
the gashed nave of Coventry fills up with rain
(another howling doodlebug of fright hurls itself
over); the church—from which, refusing to commit
the fiction of a lost belief in One True Body,
she stayed away—upholds the fabric in which her
fictions, perdurable now, cohere like fact: Lydgate
still broods, Grandcourt still threatens, and
in Mrs. Transome disappointment turns to stone.

Michelle Cliff

The Land of Look Beyond

> On the edge of each canefield or "piece" was a watch house, a tiny structure with one entry. These were used for the babies of nursing slaves who worked in the fields. An older woman was in charge of the infants and the mothers came there for feeding time.
> **tourist brochure of the Whim Great House**

A tiny structure with one entry
walls guttered with mortar
molasses   coral   sand
hold the whole thing fast.

One hundred years later
the cut limestone
sunned and salted
looks like new.

And feels like? And feels like?
I don't know.
Describe it.
Sad? Lost? Angry?
Let me get my bearings.

Outside
A tamarind tree with a dead nest in the first crotch
Dense mud construction.
Immense. The inhabitants long gone.
Hard brown pods crack underfoot
The soursweet flesh is dried.
Inedible.

Inside
One thin bench faces a blank wall.
No message from the watchwomen here.
No HELP ME carved in the mortar or the stone.
Try to capture the range—

What did their voices sound like?
What tongues? What words for day and night?
Hunger? Milk?
What songs devised to ease them?

Was there time to speak? To sing?
To the riverain goddesses
The mermaids bringing secrets
To bring down Shàngó's★ wrath.

No fatting-houses here.
Nowhere to learn the secrets
except through some new code
in spaces they will never own.

How many voices? How many drops of milk?
How many gums daubed with rum to soothe the teething
or bring on sleep?

How many breasts bore scars?
Not the sacred markings of the Carib—
but the mundane mark of the beast.

How many dropped in the field?
How many bare footfalls across the sand floor?
How many were buried?
I leave through the opening and take myself home.

*Shàngó is the Yoruba god of thunder and lightning and vengeance.

I-tie-all-my-people-together

Mo so awon enia mi po

Oshun makes of her people one
Mo so awon enia mi po

healer	destroyer of cruelty
mother	bringer of judgment
lover	excelling in tenderness
guardian	punishing foolishness

she lives at the bottom of the river
she greets the most important matter in the water

generous fury
calm intelligence
burning sweetness

she smites the belly of the liar with her bell

mistress of àshe, *of full predictive power*

she is coolness.

There is an old man standing behind me in a darkened hall.
He might be standing in the high grass of a treeless savannah.

I shut the door and turn around.

There is an old man watching me in this darkened hall.
He might be watching his cattle graze near the River Niger.

The old man and I face each other   stand exactly eye-to-eye.

He might be facing a woman come back from bartering
   firewood.

Whitened hair circles the brownness of his skull
Whitened beard fringes his soft round chin.

He is not a dream. Is he a messenger?
I do not know him. How could I have created him?
His eyes are large. He is silent as he regards me.

The old man stands   his cape over one shoulder
is made of strip-woven cloth.
He might be squatting in a marketplace in Abomey.
What has he come to tell me?

The cape he wears has colors—brown and black
   predominate—
but this is a darkened hall and all other colors are lost in its
shadows.

The old man carries a walking staff, a spear.
He might be traveling across a ridge near the Black Volta
seeking a friend.

Long, dark wood is tipped with an iron blade—dull-colored,
   oval.
The blade reaches past his right shoulder. He leans against his
staff as he regards me.

He is complete. How could he belong here?
What has brought him?

They are calling his name in some village right now.
Wondering where he has disappeared to. What would anyone
want with this old man?

There might be guns aimed at his head in Sharpeville.

I need him
The fingers of his right hand wrap around his staff.
He has come a long way to find me.

I feel an immense quiet around us.
There is not one sound. We have moved out of sound.
We are not in this house. Something holds us. We are not
in this time. We are caught somewhere. At this instant there is
nothing but us.

Stillness.
I can see by his eyes that he knows me.
That he has come all this way to tell me.

The street sounds   he is gone.

Ashe is a concept central to Yoruba belief. It is defined by Thompson as
"the power to make things happen." It is the gift of Olorun, God
Almighty.
Italicized passages are taken from a Yoruban hymn to Oshun, found in
Robert Farris Thompson.

Flash of the Spirit
(Random House, New York, 1984).

31

Lucille Clifton

poem

> them bones
> them bones will
> rise again
> them bones
> them bones will
> walk again
> them bones
> them bones will
> talk again
> now hear
> the word of The Lord.
>
> **Traditional**

atlantic is a sea of bones.
my bones.
my elegant afrikans
connecting whydah and new york,
a bridge of ivory.

seabed they call it.
in its arms my early mothers sleep.
some women leapt with babies in their arms.
some women wept and threw the babies in.

maternal armies pace the atlantic floor.
i call my name into the roar of surf
and something awful answers.

winnie song

a dark wind is blowing
the townships into town.
they have burned your house
winnie mandela
but your house has been on fire
a hundred years.
they have locked your husband
in a cage

and it has made him free.
Mandela. Mandala. Mandala
is the universe. the universe
is burning. a dark wind is blowing
the homelands into home.

album

for lucille chan hall

1. it is 1939.
    our mothers are turning our hair
    around rags.
    our mothers
    have filled our shirley temple cups.
    we drink it all.

2. 1939 again.
    our shirley temple curls.
    shirley yellow.
    shirley black.
    our colors are fading.

later we had to learn ourselves.
back across 2 oceans
into bound feet and nappy hair.

3. 1958 and 9.
    we have dropped daughters,
    afrikan and chinese.
    we think
    they will be beautiful.
    we think
    they will become themselves.

4. it is 1985.
    she is.
    she is.
    they are.

Jane Cooper

Rent

If you want my apartment, sleep in it
but let's have a clear understanding:
the books are still free agents.

If the rocking chair's arms surround you
they can also let you go,
they can shape the air like a body.

I don't want your rent, I want
a radiance of attention
like the candle's flame when we eat,

I mean a kind of awe
attending the spaces between us—
Not a roof but a field of stars.

Jittoku, Buddhist Mystic—15th Century

Everything is blowing, his
skirts are blowing, he stands
hands clasped in enormous sleeves
behind his back, at his feet a
dropped broom. The strokes of the
broom made of dry sticks and the
swoop of a few live pine needles
shiver together, his unruly
chopped-off hair and the fringes
of his girdle all are blowing
eastward. Only the corners of his
mouth defy gravity. He is laughing,
humped against the wind with his bawdy
nostrils wide he is laughing: The
moon! Old boat of the white full moon!

Conversation by the Body's Light

Out of my poverty
Out of your poverty
Out of your nakedness
Out of my nakedness
Between the swimmer in the water
And the watcher of the skies
Something is altered

Something is offered
Something is breathed
The body's radiance
Like the points of a constellation
Beckons to insight
Here is my poverty:
A body hoarded
Ridiculous in middle age
Unvoiced, unpracticed

And here is your poverty:
A prodigality
That guts its source
The self picked clean
In its shining houses

Out of my nakedness
Out of your nakedness
Between the swimmer in the skies
And the watcher from the water
Something is reached
For a moment, acknowledged
Lost—or is it shelter?
The still not-believed-in
Heartbeat of the glacier

Jayne Cortez

Big Fine Woman from Ruleville

for Fannie Lou Hamer

How to weave your web of medicinal flesh into words
cut the sutures to your circumcised name
make your deformed leg into a symbol of resistance
Big fine woman from Ruleville
great time keeper
and dangerous worker
I use this hour in my life
to eat from your spirit
dance from mouth to mouth with your holler
hold fingers together in remembrance of your sacrifices
And I have chosen to wear your riverstone eyes splashed
with Mississippi blood
and your sharecropper shoes braided with your powerful stomp
and now in your riot-stick neck smeared in charcoal burns
and in your sick and tired of being sick and tired look
and in your bones that exhausted the god of whiteness in Sun
                                        Flower county
I will push forward your precious gift of revolutionary courage
Thanks to the southern knife with terracotta teeth
magnificent ancestor
warrior friend
most beautiful sister
I kiss the mud of this moment

Acceptance Speech

And now to overcome what ?
The secretary's face
The publisher's glasses
Two intellectuals winking to
         each other across the table
A vibration of tv voices
Spectators covered with ball point pens
Pigeons waiting for Amtrak trains

Impulses sent to slash the belly
        carve out the navel
        tear down the day
        plunge into the midnight dump of dead
                        chickens
                    to overcome what?
Frivolous gestures of a woman so unnaturally bloated
i'm exhausted
Dying laugh of a man so rotten in the eyes
i hide on the first bus leaving
Stammering dirge of a child so active with fear
i tremble without trembling
exist without existing
overcome without overthrowing
and for that
i'm supposed to thank the producer for
                    making it possible
Thank some god for making it happen
Thank my sore butt for thanking you in
the combat tooth of every missing word doing
        time on this rag of discharge reflecting
                    back into repression
        back into sexual crust of
                    dazzling pigs
to say thanks for filth of rocket sweat in the vulva
Thanks for nostril feathers of metallic boogers in
blood
Thanks for rectum of imperialist flames in shit
Thanks for glow of agent orange pus in orbit
Thanks for the shivering hole of pink foam on fire
Thanks no thanks
        and don't touch it
                    ass in front of pain
                            don't
                            touch it.

Tell Me

Tell me that the plutonium sludge
in your corroded torso is all a dream

Tell me that your penis bone is not erupting
with the stench of dead ants
that your navel is not the dump site
                    of contaminated pus
that the spillage from your hard ass
is not a fallout of radioactive waste
Tell me it's a lie

Tell me it's a joke

Tell me that you don't have to fuck yourself on
the reactor core of an intense meltdown
                            to show your importance
Tell me that you have no desire
to be the first one to fuck
                into the fission of a fusion
                        of a fucking holocaust

Tell me i'm hallucinating
Tell me i'm fantasizing
Tell me i'm delirious
Tell me you know peace is better than war
that total decolonization is better than war
that elimination of hunger is better than war
that the moon merging into the shadow of the earth
                                is better than war
That night moving into day
and day moving   back into night is better than war
That the sound of the human voice in its calmness
in its shrillness
in its monumental invention of pitches
                            is better than war

that the arrival of rain
the smell of something familiar
the blood circulating in your legs
the visitation of the sun
the conjunction of rivers
the vexation of your special nerve and
hope rising from the soul of your nose
                            is better than war

Tell me that the tonnage of nuclear sweat
in your prostate gland is all a mistake
tell me that your vagina
            will not be
                    a bursting silo of blue flames
that your chest
            will not be
                    an infested swamp of vomiting mosquitos
Tell me it's a mirage
Tell me it's absurd
Tell me you really have no intention of being
a homeless   nameless   sexless piece of shit
                        somewhere over the rainbow

Tell me that you have no need to get high
                    off the fumes of a neutron bomb
Tell me that you're not going to peel off your skin
and be a psychedelic corpse in the holy water of
                        patriotic slobber
Tell me it's ridiculous
Tell me it's ludicrous

But don't tell me that you think you're immune
  because there is no immunity
No immunity to the hydrogen dust
    moving like a cloud
            of a hundred trillion infuriated rhinos
No immunity to the fireball smoker
                of abdominal organs
No immunity to the fetishes wrapped
                in uranium crates
No immunity to the downwind flames
                of invisible radiation
No immunity
  and you know it
        i know it
            the computer knows it
                everybody knows it

So tell me that you're going to pull away
    from the corrupt gluttonous controllers of profit
Tear open the condescending attitudes
                full of green ashes
Separate yourself from the solitude of stagnation
Don't tell me that you want to sink into the stink
                of exotic weapons
Don't tell me that you want to quiver into the heat
                of missile repulsion
Don't tell me that you want to disappear
            into the pessimistic past
            of your own self-interest

Tell me i'm dreaming
Tell me i'm hallucinating
Tell me i'm fantasizing
Tell me it's unthinkable
Tell me it's unrealistic
Tell me it's all in my imagination
Tell me you never heard of such a thing
Tell me it's a misunderstanding
Tell me it's not a human need
Tell me it's a crock of shit
Tell me it's propaganda
Tell me you really intend to go forward
Tell me
Tell me
Tell me

Thulani Davis

Dreamtime I
You Dog You

Pasture for Cryptograms Painting by Emilio Cruz
7″ × 7″ orlon canvas

Wings
hid by your merciless
evolution
crying up from desert
once a grassland
they may say
not in any life
time
Erzulie or the falcon
bearing a barren fruit
gorgeous
humans see to weep
soap operas or great art
smiling parodies of knowing
your self
thrown aside with the trash
your infatuation
with death & dreamtime
stay in character
you arrogant beast you
if you eat, eat
shit, shit,
sleep, sleep,
selling the light
as you know it
thrown aside with the trash
don't be nice
know your self
I'll know you by your lines
the strokes on your walls
the lapis blue of your dog
white marble eyes
implacable
you running dog you
serpent goddess
clutching the racy edge
a head

vultures
dog shadows the tomb
my face
stay in character
beast crouching
before skulls

moviestar

I
moviestar
on the highway to work
dreams of swimming 30 laps
very slowly
the traffic traps her
trucks swarm with hot drivers
pacing the asphalt
begging lights and time
they meet housewives thru windows
tractor trailers straddle the road
and everyone is really glad
they hate their jobs
and the same old exits
kids, husband, body
the moviestar yawns
practices one arm tanning
turns up the Doobie Brothers
she hates her job too
the questions are already answered
didn't we see you in the paper?
was that really you?
aren't you excited?

II
she's always excited
it's her job
to stay excited
she drives the workers crazy
they don't want to remember
their bodies, wives, or kids
how they craved for her
or something
they want to feel good
they desire to tell her she's dumb
they desire to hate the color of her
they want to go on loving money
they want to get a light
but they don't want anything lit
she wants to swim 30 laps
very slowly
pulling the pool past her feet
and all the water with it.

Angela de Hoyos

Rosario, En La Cima

Even without that engraved
wedding ring on your finger
I would know you anywhere, Rosario.
You are she who rides
the restless stag at night
when the moon gets in your eyes
and you can't sleep.

Like yours, mine is an exile
by choice; I too prefer
the cold of the páramo
to a house not a home

> —the soft pillow
> the comfortable couch
> :they become a slavehood
> to keep a woman tethered
> like a silent odalisque
> :a satellite, confined
> to a role unsung.

But you, Rosario
you have defied them
:you questioned, you denounced
those arbitrary keepers
of our souls.
And you have given us a place
—a place where woman
is a being complete
simply, as *woman*.

Here, on the mountain-top
with freedom of choice before us
your voice of oracles
defines our liberation:

> Hermanas, your attention please!
> Our assignment for today
> is the making of
> a daring new world.

> It will be autonomous
> and of our own creation.

It will spin
to no music
but our own.

Third-World Theme

          with savoring eyes
con los ojos saboreando
         and trembling fingers
y trémulous los dedos
partimos el pan
     we broke the bread
y no alcanzó para todos
        —not enough to go around—

de esta mesa alguien
se acostará con hambre
      from this table tonight
      someone will go hungry

señor presidente
      President Paleface
qué nos aconseja . . .?
     what shall we do
     for tomorrow . . .?

For Marsha

    —under the old sun
    we will know each other
    by the dust on our feet.
    Jose Flores Peregrino

in the eye of my heart, I can see her:
    the diligent artisan, committed
    with clay & sand & water
     designing, shaping, refining
      the earthen cup, warm in her hands
     —a drinking cup
the color of soft midnight, a vessel
of strength for daily wear

its pedestal is hollow
   —always an achievement

in ceramics, and denoting
the need for space
                    within space—
:a freedom only autochthonal blood
   can fully understand

she wanted to give me something
that would speak in celebration
of her/our essence of
indigenous affinity: she, Choctaw
                    I, Mexica

. . . Angela . . . here, take this cup
and whenever you drink of it
think of me ! . .

dear Marsha! Marsha Gomez,
your gift will throb forever
within these words from my/our

RAZA LOVE   RAZA NEED   RAZA EXPRESSION

esta noche, al llegarme
   la onda de tu poesía
      se abrió me corazón
         y te descubrí . . . hermana mía . . .

Toi Derricotte

the mirror poems

> Je vous livre le secret des secrets.
> Les miroirs sont les portes par
> lesquelles la Mort va et vient.
> Cocteau

Prologue:
    If she could only break the glass—
the silver is already peeled back like first skin
leaving a thin
transparent thing that floats across the ground
in front of her: this white shadow.

1 what a mirror thinks
    a mirror thinks it has no self
so it wants to be everything it sees

it also thinks everything is flat

put a bunch together
& they think they see
the back side of the moon

2 the mirror as a judge of character
    keening my appetite
on the taste of an image of myself
sharpening myself
on bones;
suddenly
i lean over its eye
& see the way i see myself

i ask it
am i fairest in all the land

it opens like a backwards lake
& throws out of its center
a woman
combing her hair
with the fingers of the dead

3 the mirror & suicide
    someday
stand before a mirror & feel
you are drowned

let
your hair spread as sweet Ophelia's did
& you will rock
back & forth
gently
like a boat in kind water

4 questions to ask a mirror
remember:
whatever you ask a mirror
it will ask back

if you ask it
what will you give me
it will ask you
what will you give me

if you ask it what is love
it will turn into a telescope
& point at you

if you ask it what is hate
it will do the same thing

if you ask it what is truth
it will break in nine pieces

if you ask it what is beauty
it will cast no reflection

if you ask it to show you the world
it will show you the eye of your mother

5 conversing with the mirror
never tell a mirror you are black
it will see you as a rainbow
never tell a mirror you are white
it will make you disappear
in fact a mirror doesn't care
what color you are

never tell a mirror
how old you are
under 20
you draw a blank
over 40   it stares

never cry in front of a mirror
it gets cruel

if a mirror doesn't trust you
it squints

if a mirror hates you
it speaks in a high-pitched voice

if a mirror calls you long distance
don't accept charges   hang up

never run from a mirror
it always leaves a friend outside

never have sex with a mirror
you will have in-grown children

don't take money from a mirror
there are strings

if you must converse with a mirror
say to it: you're pretty
& won't get broken

that gives you
7 years

6 *the mirror & time*
the mirror IS NOT immortal
in fact it only has nine lives:

the first one is a thief
the second a baker
the third plays the harpsichord
the fourth lives in the iron-bound
section of newark &
eats pork sausage
the fifth predictably drinks
the sixth goes into the convent
but the seventh (this gets better)
marries her father
& humps up like a camel
the eighth cries a lot and ZAP
changes into a writer

7 *the mirror & metamorphosis*
the eye   in the mirror   is the mirror   of the eye

8 *the mirror & the new math*
inside the mirror
opens up like the number zero
you swim around in there
bob up
& drown
like the rat in Wonderland's flood.
your tail would like to hook a reason,

but you keep coming
face to face
breast to breast
with yourself.

you fall backwards & away, even
think that you are lost
In Oceanic O,

but you are still
pinned to an inverse.

9 the mirror as a silent partner
    the mirror never talks
    it is always astounded
    with its O mouth open
    & everything falling in

Epilogue:
    Always straining toward her image, the girl
    let go.

    Tentacles of light
    unlocked
    like hooks of parasite

    & she came back
    in dark so dark,

she cannot see by sight

Diane di Prima

Excerpts from Loba

from Ave

O lost moon sisters
crescent in hair, sea underfoot do you wander
in blue veil, in green leaf, in tattered shawl do you wander

with goldleaf skin, with flaming hair do you wander
on Avenue A, on Bleecker Street do you wander
on Rampart Street, on Fillmore Street do you wander
      with flower wreath, with jeweled breath do you wander

   footprints
     shining mother of pearl
           behind you
moonstone eyes
    in which the crescent moon

with gloves, with hat, in rags, in fur, in beads
under the waning moon, hair streaming in black rain
wailing with stray dogs, hissing in doorways
shadows you are, that fall on the crossroads, highways

jaywalking do you wander
spitting do you wander
mumbling and crying do you wander
aged and talking to yourselves
with roving eyes do you wander
hot for quick love do you wander
weeping your dead

      naked you walk
      swathed in long robes you walk
      swaddled in death shroud you walk
      backwards you walk

        hungry
        hungry
        hungry

     shrieking I hear you
     singing I hear you
     cursing I hear you
     praying I hear you

you lie with the unicorn
you lie with the cobra
you lie in the dry grass
you lie with the yeti
you flick long cocks of satyrs with your tongue

      you are armed
      you drive chariots
      you tower above me
      you are small
      you cower on hillsides
      out of the winds

pregnant you wander
barefoot you wander
battered by drunk men you wander

      you kill on steel tables
      you birth in black beds
            fetus you tore out stiffens in snow
            it rises like new moon
            you moan in your sleep

digging for yams you wander
looking for dope you wander
playing with birds you wander
chipping at stone you wander

I walk the long night seeking you
I climb the sea crest seeking you
I lie on the prairie, batter at stone gates
calling your names

you are coral
you are lapis and turquoise
your brain curls like shell
you dance on hills

      hard–substance–woman you whirl
      you dance on subways
      you sprawl in tenements
      children lick at your tits

you are the hills, the shape and color of mesa
you are the tent, the lodge of skins, the hogan
the buffalo robes, the quilt, the knitted afghan
you are the cauldron and the evening star
you rise over the sea, you ride the dark

I move within you, light the evening fire
I dip my hand in you and eat your flesh
you are my mirror image and my sister
you disappear like smoke on misty hills
you lead me thru dream forest on horseback
large gypsy mother, I lean my head on your back

      I am you
      and I must become you

I have been you
and I must become you
I am always you
I must become you

> *ay-a*
> *ay-a ah*
> *ay-a*
> *ay-a ah ah*
> *maya ma maya ma*
> *om star mother ma om*
> *maya ma ah*

from Part II

The day lay like a pearl on her lap
she licked at it w / the edges of her brain
The day shone in her lap like a promise
of lotuses sprouting from warm worm-eaten mud
but the sand under her toes was dry
dry the dust in her hair
dry & smooth her cunt like lapis lazuli
between her legs, close lapis cunt closegrained,
                      & veined
w/ silver; the day sat
in her fingers like a jewel she turned
in the failing light, the sun
falling into her sea turned
smoky quartz day to a yellow
                           diamond, a topaz
and then to apache tears the starlight
broke on, as on the waves

      ★   ★   ★

where did it
come from, were there
any more, where it
came from, had she
remembered to
pay for it

rhinestones in her ears shook
sideways, glittering, rattled
a little, she sat down
on the curb, with a small boy
ate a tomato

The Ruses: A Coyote Tale

from Part VI/The Seven Joys of the Virgin

    Sometimes you take up the trap &
run with the metal between yr teeth,
    At times it is better to chew off
your leg.
    You have in this case to consider
the trail of blood.
    Sometimes for weeks it is better
not to eat, the meat is poisoned, but
you wait it out
    knowing the creatures are not
consistent, they forget. Or they will
move on. It is hard to explain this
to the cubs.
    You keep downwind, stick to
the water; journey in thick mist
or at the dark of the moon.

    There come the safe times when
we congregate in the snow,
    under large barren trees & each
of us is a flame.
    an offering to the moon.
    At such times it is unnecessary
to sing.

The Loba Recovers the Memory of a Mare

from Part VII

    small hooves
    the ankles fragile
    unsteady
    not rooted here

    the eyes
    anxious
    eyes of a doe
    who has been hunted
    but not w / in recent
    memory

who walked across America behind gaunt violent yogis
& died o-d'ing in methadone jail
scarfing the evidence

or destitute in Fiji wiring home for comfort
destroyed among oil lamps Morocco seeking dead fingers
old man in Afghani jail / pregnant barefoot & whoring
    who did we pray
    who did we pray to then

laid out flowerless in abandoned basement
blue stiff & salt injection
just out of reach
wrote lipstick "save yourself" on tin rail of furnished
    room bed
eloped w / white slaver & died Indiana of unmentioned griefs
or in love again peaceful scrawled candlesmoke "there is
    salvation" triumphant on borrowed ceiling
while friends coughed in the kitchen

who left tapestries, evidence, baby bottle behind in Vancouver

& hitched to Seattle for the mushroom season
trailing welfare checks & stolen money orders
Chicago gangster in earrings who minded the baby

who gathered reed grass for the wicki-up, eating
    horsemeat steaks in Colorado dusk
the painted hills bucking & neighing, it was her ankles

    were slender
    it was her eyes
    were tired

oatmeal & grits while the old man
    naked in bed / read Bible / jerked off
& who was the whore of Babylon in the
    kerosene lamp of yr childhood?

It was her skirt
was greasy
it was her skirt
was graceful
it was her skirt
you clung to, till she fell
you fell

    & who now remembers her hands
working dye into cotton
slant of her green eyes / Sagamore cafeteria

who has tears for girls now on Route One, the babies
wrapped in a scarf/ the green
    always further north
    further than you can walk

her ankles fragile
unrooted, she walks
into the Wind

Rita Dove

Canary

for Michael S. Harper

Billie Holiday's burned voice
had as many shadows as lights,
a mournful candelabra against a sleek piano,
the gardenia her signature under that ruined face.

(Now you're cooking, drummer to bass,
magic spoon, magic needle.
Take all day if you have to
with your mirror and your bracelet of song.)

Fact is, the invention of women under siege
has been to sharpen love in the service of myth.

If you can't be free, be a mystery.

Parsley

1   The Cane Fields
There is a parrot imitating spring
in the palace, its feathers parsley green.
Out of the swamp the cane appears

to haunt us, and we cut it down. El General
searches for a word; he is all the world
there is. Like a parrot imitating spring,

we lie down screaming as rain punches through
and we come up green. We cannot speak an R—
out of the swamp, the cane appears

and then the mountain we call in whispers *Katalina*.
The children gnaw their teeth to arrowheads.
There is a parrot imitating spring.

El General has found his word: *perejil*.
Who says it, lives. He laughs, teeth shining
out of the swamp. The cane appears

in our dreams, lashed by wind and streaming.
And we lie down. For every drop of blood
there is a parrot imitating spring.
Out of the swamp the cane appears.

2   *The Palace*
The word the general's chosen is parsley.
It is fall, when thoughts turn
to love and death; the general thinks
of his mother, how she died in the fall
and he planted her walking cane at the grave
and it flowered, each spring stolidly forming
four-star blossoms. The general

pulls on his boots, he stomps to
her room in the palace, the one without
curtains, the one with a parrot
in a brass ring. As he paces he wonders
Who can I kill today. And for a moment
the little knot of screams
is still. The parrot, who has traveled

all the way from Australia in an ivory
cage, is coy as a widow, practicing
spring. Ever since the morning
his mother collapsed in the kitchen
while baking skull-shaped candies
for the Day of the Dead, the general
has hated sweets. He orders pastries
brought up for the bird; they arrive

dusted with sugar on a bed of lace.
The knot in his throat starts to twitch;
he sees his boots the first day in battle
splashed with mud and urine
as a soldier falls at his feet amazed—
how stupid he looked!—at the sound
of artillery. *I never thought it would sing*
the soldier said, and died. Now

the general sees the fields of sugar
cane, lashed by rain and streaming.
He sees his mother's smile, the teeth
gnawed to arrowheads. He hears
the Haitians sing without R's
as they swing the great machetes:
Katalina, they sing, *Katalina*,

mi madle, mi amol en muelte. God knows
his mother was no stupid woman; she
could roll an R like a queen. Even
a parrot can roll an R! In the bare room
the bright feathers arch in a parody
of greenery, as the last pale crumbs
disappear under the blackened tongue. Someone

calls out his name in a voice
so like his mother's, a startled tear
splashes the tip of his right boot.
My mother, my love in death.
The general remembers the tiny green sprigs
men of his village wore in their capes
to honor the birth of a son. He will
order many, this time, to be killed

for a single, beautiful word.

After Reading *Mickey in the Night Kitchen* for the Third Time Before Bed

"I'm in the milk and
the milk's in me! . . . I'm Mickey!"

My daughter spreads her legs
to find her vagina:
hairless, this mistaken
bit of nomenclature
is what a stranger cannot touch
without her yelling. She demands
to see mine and momentarily
we're a lopsided star
among the spilled toys,
my prodigious scallops
exposed to her neat cameo.

And yet the same glazed
tunnel, layered sequences.
She is three; that makes this
innocent. *We're pink!*
she shrieks, and bounds off.

Every month she wants
to know where it hurts and
what the wrinkled string means
between my legs. *This is good blood*
I say, but that's wrong, too.
How to tell her that it's what makes us—
black mother, cream child.
That we're in the pink
and the pink's in us.

Carolyn Forché

The Memory of Elena

We spend our morning
in the flower stalls counting
the dark tongues of bells
that hang from ropes waiting
for the silence of an hour.
We find a table, ask for *paella*,
cold soup and wine, where a calm
light trembles years behind us.

In Buenos Aires only three
years ago, it was the last time his hand
slipped into her dress, with pearls
cooling her throat and bells like
these, chipping at the night—

As she talks, the hollow
clopping of a horse, the sound
of bones touched together.
The *paella* comes, a bed of rice
and *camarones*, fingers and shells,
the lips of those whose lips
have been removed, mussels
the soft blue of a leg socket.

This is not *paella*, this is what
has become of those who remained
in Buenos Aires. This is the ring
of a rifle report on the stones,
her hand over her mouth,
her husband falling against her.

These are the flowers we bought
this morning, the dahlias tossed
on his grave and bells
waiting with their tongues cut out
for this particular silence.

Because One Is Always Forgotten

In Memoriam, José Rudolfo Viera 1939–1981: El Salvador

When Viera was buried we knew it had come to an end,
his coffin rocking into the ground like a boat or a cradle.

I could take my heart, he said, and give it to a *campesino*
and he would cut it up and give it back:

you can't eat heart in those four dark
chambers where a man can be kept years.

A boy soldier in the bone-hot sun works his knife
to peel the face from a dead man

and hang it from the branch of a tree
flowering with such faces.

The heart is the toughest part of the body.
Tenderness is in the hands.

On Returning to Detroit

Over the plum snow, the train's blonde smoke,
dawn coming into Detroit but like Bratislava

the icy undersides of the train, the passengers
asleep on one another and those who cannot

pace the aisles touching seats to steady themselves
and between the cars their hair is silvered

by the fine ice that covers everything; a man
slamming his hand into a morning paper

a woman who has so rubbed her bright grey eyes
during grief that all she has seen can be seen in them

the century, of which twenty years are left,
several wars, a fire of black potatoes

and maybe a moment when across a table
she was loved and as a much younger woman

wet her fingertip and played the bells of empty
glasses of wine, impossible not to imagine her

doing that, drawing the shade and then in its ochre
light, the first button of his shirt, the rest

the plants boarded up along the wide black river,
the spools of unraveling light that are the rails

the domed Greek church, the glass hopes of the city

beside one another; the man whose clothes

he carries in a pillowcase, the woman whose old love
walks into her eyes each morning and with a pole

lowers the awnings over the shop stalls of fruit.

Celia Gilbert

Voices

For you, having your first child at 38

Ellen/Not lost/but gone before
Mary/Gone to rest/She is not dead/but sleeping

August heat swaddles the cemetery
but the slant of light warns how we tip
to autumn now. Gently, I put my hand on your belly,
five months full, hard as a crystal ball.
No child will ever quicken in me again.
I called you my Virgo sister once
born on the same day, ten years after me,
years that marked us as if
we came from different countries.

Helen/Beloved wife of Henry Stevens
She always made home happy

"I feel the baby kicking now," you say.
I'd forgotten your voice, husky and childlike.
I've forgotten many things. The distance I am
from your happiness measures the time for me—
the miles I must travel back to the woman
I was, strolling under the trees, feeling
the baby in me like a buckler
against the world's woes; dreaming
of a Republic where I would set every wrong
to right, raising the child at my knee.
Then, locked in service to that myth
as exigent as any stepmother's commands,
what could I understand of your talk
of protest, struggle—the vision
you pursued? You, free to act,
you changed our times and I am changed
because of you.

I envy you, watching you read
the Memorial to the Union.
Here the Civil War lies buried
under a sphinx with the wide, blank eyes
of a coin. Had we been born to the South, I
would have acquiesced, you
would have crossed in the awful dark

60

with the slaves, over the rivers
and divides, to give them life.

Your cheeks have hollowed; I see
some gray hair. In two years, you'll be forty.
Have you envied me for giving birth?
Your shapeless shape that antedates
all history confronts me.
How does a bird refuse to know
its wings? Only a few have ever
denied this certain power within
to gamble on greater knowledge.

Too late to tell you now of terrors
over a sick child, or rage at an adolescent
that shattered me with guilt, and the utter
loneliness of responsibilities never
fully shared. I want to forget myself,
the madwoman trying to get pregnant,
my life condensed to a castaway's vision
fixed on a speck.

I remember on a Georgia back road, a tortoise,
taking no notice of me, her time come,
in a pit of her making in the hot, gritty sand.
I knelt watching. The leathery brow wrinkled,
it seemed, in pain. I heard the hoarse expelling
of breath through the tiny skull holes
of her fierce beak.

Dogs, or a car could have killed her,
but nothing could have disconnected
the gravity that held her ejecting, one
by one, (I counted as they came) nine glowing
white almond-shapes—behind their walls
a faint pulsation of the rose of living flesh.

Then, kicking back-legs, she showered sand
over her eggs and filled the space
in slow motions—this ritual—as though
I'd been told to sort out seed with only stumps
for hands, or commanded to swim in mud.
Her time, set against theirs until, the pit filled,
she dragged her body over it, obliterating
her traces. And shocked me, as she stretched up
on wiry legs and lumbered off. How could she go?

> *Children of Peter and Lavinia Stone*
> *John, 3 months; Infant, 11 days;*
> *John Henry, 2 months; Anne, 8 yrs, 6 months*

You stand where I once stood.
We are connected beyond the grave
to those who are taken, but the ties
between ourselves and children grown
are slack. If I had *known*. What can

61

we *know*? You went to prison trusting
in your beliefs. If I spoke, you would only
hear me saying *avoid pain*.
Turning to me, you smile, filled with light.
As men go to war—ignorant, foolhardy, vainglorious,
brave—so women, to motherhood.

A Private Life

Not every man can own as Tomas does
an island, a wife, her dog, and a shark;
can claim as his the hoops
of breath-lifting, silver flying-fish
rising to praise the evening star.

Knock of night gecko on wall,
throat inflating to freckled balloon.
Clack of palmettoes in the wind,
times a frenzy.

Moon, of course, watches.
Days have turned over; years
fly above the head of Inez
hunched under Tomas' blows.

Trapped in a cove, the shark
answers his call. Tomas applauds
the teeth unstitching like a scar
as it lunges to eat the dogs and cats
he buys from passing fishermen.
Beer in hand, he notes
red stains dissolve into blue sky.

Night fragrance, frangipani so creamy
Inez longs for the wax tapers, the cool high churches
they left behind in Spain. Without child,
friends, Tomas' fame as a painter,
after a time how easy to forget history,
nothing but dawn's daily gauntlet,
heart lurching into fear,
and the small dog, Tina, at her heels.

For long hours, Inez and dog huddle
under green canopies. "Try not to think,"
she whispers to Tina.
He, hat pushed over his forehead, eye squinting,
he knows exactly how angry he is, failure
eats him like a yaw.

It hadn't always been this way.
She runs before each moment seeking

the charming Tomas she knew. Feels
her hopes rise most after each beating,
sure he will return, hold her
in his arms, understand.
Begs the Virgin to heal his soul.

At the cove, the shark circles round and round
or hovers on the bottom, sated,
a fallen shadow. The Evil One.
She warns the dog never to go near
that water. "Promise me."
Tina cocks her head, wet nose
sniffs the hollow of Inez' hand.

In the house—his old paintings everywhere.
Could he have been the one to paint
those flowers, people, pets?
Inez tries not to hear an axe thud,
but trembles when her hand must slice
into the mango's orange flesh.

Dreaming of Cordoba's white walls,
she touches a cross of carnations
that oozes to mud.
Binoculars on the mainland,
watching women hang out the wash
she looks for a message in such blankness.

Shrinks in his sight, whimpers
when spoken to. Crouches, wordless,
the day she finds Tina, swung on a rope,
dangled before the shark;
sees it bite the dog in half,
sees her utterly disappear.
Then a voice says, "You have the right."

That night she prays he'll sleep.
goes empty as the axe comes down,
pulling weak arms with it.
One slash at the neck, the axe is home.
She doesn't even hear it scrape on bone.

His head, half-lowered eyes,
mouth ajar, she saves, to explain
why she hadn't freed him before,
and slowly throws the rest
piece by piece, to the shark.
It's beautiful the way any living creature is.
How wrong she was to think it evil.

Lot's Wife

hibakusha: (hi bak̄ sha), explosion-afflicted person. The term coined
by the Japanese to signify those who were exposed to the radiation of
atomic bombs in Hiroshima and Nagasaki.

The moment I saw the strangers at the door,
men, without women, I was afraid.
I begged Lot not to take them in.
Muffled in dusty cloaks
they accepted hospitality
as if they were superior beings.
They were too beautiful—
faced hard and polished—
the light couldn't enter them,
it fell away, baffled.
But Lot was impressed by their authority,
he loved authority, loved
to use it. The men, we
thought they were men then,
they didn't care for us.
You could see they had a job to do
and that was all. They were looking
at us but thinking about the job.

> "Sweeney was like most bomber pilots who have
> formed a defensive armor about their particular role in
> war. Their function is to drop bombs on targets not on
> people. Were they to think otherwise, to be ordered to
> drop a bomb on say, 2,567 men, women, and children,
> they would probably go mad. A target was a different
> matter. . . ."

Lot and the strangers talked about good and evil
while our daughters and I served them
at table. And Lot bowed low when they said
that he was a God-fearing man who would never
do anything wicked like his neighbors.

I knew my neighbors,
women like myself, going to the well,
weaving and spinning,
raising the family.
The little boys were noisy,
dirty, and quick,
the little girls, shy, quieter,
but sturdy.

> ". . . girls, very young girls, not only with their clothes
> torn off but with their skin peeled off as well. I thought
> should there be a hell this was it—the Buddhist hell
> where we were taught people who could not attain
> salvation always went."

I saw the strangers look at our daughters
not as men look at women
but as we might look at dumb brutes—
no, not even that—for often we recognize
ourselves in their uncomprehending
helplessness. They simply looked
but did not see.

> "The most impressive thing was the expression in
> people's eyes . . . their eyes looking for someone to
> come and help them. The eyes—the emptiness—the
> helpless expression were something I will never
> forget . . . they looked at me with very great expectation
> staring right through me."

While we feasted the strangers,
the city hummed outside our doors,
the buzzing of the hive, moving,
agitating. Most people were like us
busy with small schemes. Lot called
our city wicked because he abhorred
the men in it who loved men and the women
who loved women, practices of love
he held unclean, claiming
Jews were different from other people.
But our city was like any other city.
And there were violent gangs of men
who raped men, and that seemed to many
especially horrible. When women were raped
that was wrong, they said,
but there was no special horror to it.
Then came the screams of drunks,
the obscene cries, the beating
at our doors.

And they called unto Lot,
and said unto him, Where are
the men which came in to thee
this night? bring them out
unto us, that we may know
them.

And Lot went out at the
door unto them, and shut the
door after him,

And said, I pray you,
brethren, do not so wickedly.

Behold now, I have two
daughters which have not known
man; let me, I pray you, bring
them out unto you, and do ye to
them as is good in your eyes:
only unto these men do nothing;
for therefore came they under
the shadow of my roof.

Dishonor and shame await those who
behave dishonorably.
We owed the guests at our table protection,
that was the custom,
but how could Lot offer
our virgin daughters to the mob?
He took the side of the angels—
for so they later revealed themselves—
or did he take the side of the men out there?

> "Sweeney's regular plane, *The Great Artiste*, named by
> the crew in honor of the bombardier's technique with a
> bombsight and the opposite sex, had already been
> outfitted with special instruments."

"Take my daughters, but not
the strangers within my gates—,"
words spoken with high seriousness.
The house of Lot was only Lot,
we were chattels and goods.
We women were his animals to breed.
Why didn't he offer himself to the men?
The strangers smiled.
They had their orders, and their secret
knowledge: God was created in the image of man,
him only.
The rape of women and children
is sanctioned.
Our lives were spared,
because of Lot's godliness.

> ". . . all had skin blackened by burns . . . no hair . . . at a
> glance you couldn't tell whether you were looking at
> them from in front or in back. They had their arms
> bent . . . and their skin—not only on their hands but on
> their faces and bodies, too—hung down . . . like
> walking ghosts they didn't look like people of this
> world."

We covered our heads,
my weeping daughters and I, and ran
with Lot and the strangers through the blinding
light that tore
and shattered and broke in a rain of fire and ash.

> "I climbed Hijiyama Mountain and looked down. I saw
> that Hiroshima had disappeard . . . Hiroshima had
> become an empty field."

My neighbor was gone. I remembered her,
worn with children, disagreeable,
her harassed look, bent back,
how she came one day when my daughter
was sick, with a special broth.
"Take it, it might help."

With every step my blood
congealed with unshed tears;
my body thickened.
For what were we saved?
To turn our backs on slaughter
and forget? To worship
the power that spared our lives?

Those who died are my children now,
my other children, destroyed in the fire,
neighbors, women and their young,
the animals, the green of our simple
gardens.
How can I spit out
the bitter root I gnaw, foraged from the rubble,
more sour than the apple, the knowledge
of what power rules our lives,
the evil that knows but does not care,
that values men at nothing, and women less,
behemoth in love with death
and willing, to that end, to extinguish
even itself to celebrate its own spending?

The stench of flesh my skin breathes in
cannot be washed away.
What life could I have surviving
the second's flash that revealed
the sight of the world as it is?
Seared and defiled, scorched
and silenced, I turn back,
refusing to live God's lies,
and will my body, transfixed by grief,
to rise in vigil
over the ashen cities.

Melinda Goodman

Body Work

A woman I love carries
a bag too heavy
she can never decide
what to leave behind
books, papers, clothes, cookies
it takes her nine minutes
to find a pen that works
I can help her pull
her tight shoulder gently
out of her locked socket
feel her back ribs release
loosen the muscles
down the length of her arm
find the hand inside the fist

A woman I know screams
as together we work the terror
from the backs of her exposed
white legs
the rage from her thighs
remembers straps lashed
across them
like escaped snakes from the belt loops
of her father's tan pants
the wooden spoons
that stirred her soup
were the same that left welts
where they landed flat and wide
as her eyes   and as red

A man comes to me
he has eyes like a cross
between a Saint Bernard
and Robert F. Kennedy
fooled by his outward appearance
I use all my strength
to lift him off the ground
but he is light and without roots
his body yearns for other planets
I have to grab hold quick
before his head flies
through the ceiling

A handsome young man
with a reconstructed face
the only person I know
whose head went through
the windshield of a car
from the outside to the inside
scars from his broken legs
scars from his broken arms
a hand once crushed
still won't close right
he wades through his days
with a low grade fever
stars in B-grade horror
movies that play all
the local theaters   tells me
he's the only one
that doesn't die in the end

A woman whose knees
are too weak for her body
spends too much money
on underpants and bras
hates her job
hates her apartment
faithfully mourns
for the woman who left her
faithfully goes to her sister's
engagement party in florida
comes back too sun burned
to be touched
can spread her legs wider than
anyone I work on
likes to tap dance
loves to sing
we walk down the street
singing Leader of the Pack

A woman I love
has a body that trembles
generating too much heat
to sleep against in the summer
her eyes move back and forth constantly
involuntarily
like a cat clock on the wall
with a diamond bow tie
and tail that swings
slowly she is remembering
being raped as a child

A woman I love
is six feet tall
she gets hot flashes
and night sweats
smokes cigarettes and coffee

and has beautiful long fingers
"piano hands" her mother called them
and warned her to protect
them
like she protected herself from
her mother's blows
turning her piano hands
into shields repeating
over and over "I'm sorry
I'm sorry . . . I'll never do it
again" never knowing what
she'd done
piano hands dusting her mother's
four poster sick bed after school
"And if I die, it's your fault!",
her mother screamed
and died.

I Am Married to Myself

I got married on the great lawn
one day after work
it was a beautiful affair
I wore beads around my neck   my ankles
beads around my waist   coming down my back
green, purple, blue   red and yellow   beads
I was nervous   wondering
would I run out on me at the last minute?
Not show up or refuse to take the vows?
I looked at my mother
standing to the left of me
I saw tears in the corners
of her eyes and mouth
She had on the lavender print dress
the one she wore at my sixth grade graduation
when I played the clarinet
I looked at my father
standing to the right of me
and my brother and sisters all around me
I looked at my friends   it was the last time
I saw any of them   before we cut the ice
cream cake with a little statue of me   on top

The dancers and poets were warming up
in a circle on the grass
near the caravan they had arrived in
Tents and flowers were pitched
all around the field

There was a sixteen piece salsa band
and nobody else came down
to the lake that day because coyotes
were stationed at all the roadways
within a mile circumference of the land
which belonged to my great aunt   the sky
was blue   hoo hoo
and I saw you   whoa
standing against a pine tree
off to the side
there to watch your old girlfriend
give herself away   I could've laughed
but it was my day   hey
I wasn't about   to break
the seriosity of the occasion
just because you saw fit to stumble
into my per-if-feral vision
I kept my eyes on the lake
and my hand turning my new gold
ring around and around
in the palm of my hand
I chose one with an amethyst
the tranquil gem   cool and clear
swallow of water whenever I want it

But now for the ceremony
I wrote the vows myself
all about how I will never leave me
I will love   cherish   and obey
and if it comes down to that
from dust to dust   dirt to dirt
water to water   mud to blood
thicker than water   thicker than wood
thicker than flowers, thorns, and scissors
paper around rock   rock crushes scissors
scissors cut match   match burns paper
rock   scissors   paper   match

I will always love me   I will never leave me
they're gonna have to work
to get   me

Judy Grahn

Talkers in a dream doorway

You leaned your body in the doorway
(it was a dim NY hall)
I was leaving as usual—on my way.
You had your head cocked to the side
in your most intelligent manner
eyes glistening   with provocation,
gaze direct as always,
and more, as though wanting something,
as though I could have bent and kissed you
like a lover
and nothing social would have changed,
no one minded, no one bothered.
I can't testify to your intention.

I can only admit to my temptation.

Your intensity dazed me, so matter of fact
as though I could have leaned my denser body into yours,
in that moment while the cab waited
traffic roaring nine flights down
as well as in my ears,
both of us with lovers of our own
and living on each end of a large continent.
We were raised in vastly different places,
yet speak this uncanny similar tongue.
Some times we're different races,
certainly we're different classes,
yet our common bonds and common graces,
common wounds and destinations
keep us closer than some married folks.

I admit I have wanted to touch your face, intimately.

Supposing that I were to do this awful
act, this breach of all our lovers' promises—in reality—
this tiny, cosmic infidelity: I believe our lips would first be
tentative, then hardened in a rush of feeling, unity
such as we thought could render up the constellations AND our
daily lives, justice, equality AND freedom,
give us worldly definition
AND the bread of belonging. In the eye of my imagination
I see my fingers curled round the back of your head
as though it were your breast

and I were pulling it to me.
As though your head were your breast
and I were pulling it to me.

I admit, I have wanted to possess your mind.

I leaned forward to say goodbye,
aware of your knuckle possibly digging a tunnel
through my thigh, of the whole shape of your body as
an opening, a doorway to the heart.
Both of us with other lives to lead
still sure why we need so much to join,
and do join with our eyes on every
socially possible occasion.
More than friends, even girl friends,
more than comrades, surely,
more than workers with the same bent,
and more than fellow magicians
exchanging recipes for a modern brand of golden spit.

I admit we have already joined more than physically.

The cab's horn roars.
You smile, or part your lips as if to welcome how I'd just
slip in there, our tongues nodding together,
talking inside each other's mouth for a change,
as our upper bodies talked that night we danced together.
Your face was wine-flushed, and foolish; my desire selfish,
pushing you beyond your strength.
You paid for it later, in pain, you said.
I forget you are older, and fragile. I forget your arthritis.
I paid later in guilt, though not very much.
I loved holding you so close, your ear pressed to my ear.
I wanted to kiss you then but I didn't dare
lest I spoil the real bonding we were doing there.

I admit I have wanted to possess my own life.

Our desire is that we want to talk of really important things,
and words come so slowly, eons of movement
squirt them against our gums. Maybe once in ten years a sentence
actually flashes out, altering everything in its path.
Flexing our tongues into each other's dreams, we want to
suck a new language, strike a thought into being, out of the old
fleshpot. That rotten old body of our long submersion. We sense
the new idea can be a dance of all kinds of women,
one we seek with despair and desire
and exaltation; are willing to pay for
with all-consuming passion, AND those tiny boring paper cuts.
I never did lean down to you that day.
I said goodbye with longing and some confusion.

I admit to wanting a sword AND a vision.

I doubt I will ever kiss you in that manner.
I doubt I will ever stop following you around, wanting to.
This IS our love, this stuff

pouring out of us, and if this mutual desire is
some peculiar ether-marriage
among queens, made of the longing of women
to really love each other, made of dreams
and needs larger than all of us,
we may not know what to do
with it yet but at least
we've got it,
we're in the doorway.
We've got it right here, between us,

(admit it) on the tip of our tongues.

Helen in Hollywood

When she goes to Hollywood
she is an angel.

She writes in red red lipstick
on the window of her body,
long for me, oh need me!
Parts her lips like a lotus.

Opening night she stands, poised
on her carpet, luminescent,
young men humming
all around her. She is flying.
Her high heels are wands, her
furs electric. Her bracelets
flashing. How completely
dazzling her complexion,
how vibrant her hair and eyes,
how brilliant the glow that spreads
four full feet around her.

She is totally self conscious
self contained
self centered,
caught in the blazing central eye
of our attention.

We infuse her.
Fans, we wave at her
like handmaids, unabashedly,
we crowd on tiptoe pressed together
just to feel the fission of the star
that lives on earth,
the bright, the angel sun
the luminescent glow of someone
other than we.

Look! Look! She is different.
Medium for all our energy
as we pour it through her.
Vessel of light.
Her flesh is like flax,
a living fiber.
She is the symbol of our dreams and fears
and bloody visions, all
our metaphors for living in America.

Harlowe, Holiday, Monroe

Helen
when she goes to Hollywood
she is the fire for all purposes.

Her flesh is like dark wax, a candle.
She is from any place or class.
"That's the one," we say in instant recognition,
because our breath is taken by her beauty,
or what we call her beauty.

She is glowing from every pore.
we adore her. we imitate and rob her
adulate   envy
admire   neglect
scorn. leave alone
invade, fill
ourselves with her.
we love her, we say
and if she isn't careful
we may even kill her.

Opening night
she lands on her carpet,
long fingered hands
like divining rods
bobbing and drawing the strands
of our attention,
as limousine drivers in blue jackets
stand on the hoods of their cars
to see the angel, talking

Davis, Dietrich, Wood
Tyson, Taylor, Gabor
Helen, when she goes to Hollywood
to be a walking star,
to be an actor

She is far more than a product
of Max Factor,
Max Factor didn't make her
though the make-up helps us
see what we would like
to take her for

her flesh is like glass,
a chandelier
a mirror

Harlowe, Holiday, Monroe
Helen
when she went to Hollywood
to be an angel

And it is she and not we
who is different

She who marries the crown prince
who leads the processional dance,
she who sweeps eternally
down the steps
in her long round gown.
A leaping, laughing leading lady,
she is our flower.
It is she who lies strangled
in the bell tower;
she who is monumentally drunk and suicidal
or locked waiting in the hightower,
she who lies sweating with the vicious jungle fever,
who leaps from her blue window
when he will, if he will, leave her

it is she and not we
who is the lotus

It is she with the lilies in her hair
and a keyboard beside her,
the dark flesh glowing

She whose wet lips nearly swallow
the microphone, whose whiskey voice
is precise and sultry and overwhelming,
she who is princess and harlequin,
athlete and moll and whore and lady,
goddess of the silver screen
the only original American queen

and Helen
when she was an angel
when she went to Hollywood

in the place where

in the place where
her breasts come together
two thumbs' width of

channel ride my
eyes to anchor
hands to angle
in the place where
her legs come together
I said "you smell like the
ocean" and lay down my tongue
beside the dark tooth edge
of sleeping
"swim" she told me and I
did, I did

Asking for Ruthie

you know her hustle
you know her white legs
flicker among headlights
and her eyes pick up the wind
while the fast hassle of living
ticks off her days
you know her ways

you know her hustle
you know her lonely pockets
lined with tricks
turned and forgotten
the men like mice hide
under her mind
lumpy, bigeyed
you know her pride

you know her blonde arms cut
by broken nickels in
hotelrooms and by razors of
summer lightning on the road
but you know the wizard
highway, no resisting so
she moves, she is forever missing
get her a stopping place
before the night slides dirty
fingers under her eyelids and
the weight of much bad kissing
breaks that ricepaper face

sun cover her, earth,
make love to Ruthie
stake her to hot lunches in the wheat fields
make bunches of purple ravens
fly out in formation, over her eyes

and let her newest lovers
be gentle as women
and longer lasting

from Confrontations with the Devil
in the Form of Love

My name is Judith, meaning
She Who Is Praised
I do not want to be called praised
I want to be called The Power of Love.

If Love means protect then whenever I do not
defend you
I cannot call my name Love.
if Love means rebirth then when I see us
dead on our feet
I cannot call my name Love.
if Love means provide & I cannot
provide for you
why would you call my name Love?

do not mistake my breasts
for mounds of potatoes
or my belly for a great roast duck.
do not take my lips for a streak of luck
nor my neck for an appletree,
do not believe my eyes are a warm swarm of bees;
do not get Love mixed up with me.

Don't misunderstand my hands
for a church with a steeple,
open the fingers & out come the people;
nor take my feet to be acres of solid brown earth,
or anything else of infinite worth
to you, my brawny turtledove;
do not get me mixed up with Love.

not until we have ground we call our own
to stand on
& weapons of our own in hand
& some kind of friends around us
will anyone ever call our name Love,
& then when we do we will all call ourselves
grand, muscley names:
the Protection of Love,
the Provision of Love & the
Power of Love.
until then, my sweethearts,
let us speak simply of

romance, which is so much
easier and so much less
than any of us deserve.

Susan Griffin

Prayer for Continuation

1
There is a record
I wish to make here.
A life.
And not this life alone
but the thread
which keeps shining
like gold floss woven into cloth
which catches your eyes
and you are won over.

Kyrie Eleison
Baruch atah
Hosana   adonai
Omne Padme   Gloria
Nam Myo-Ho
Renge Kyo
Galan
galancillo.
Do you love
this world?

Where is the point I can enter?
Where is the place I can touch?

Let me tell you
I am so serious
and taking aim
like a woman with a bow
eyes looking silently
at each space between the trees
for movement.

2
I cannot begin now.
I do not wish to write these numbers
on this page here.
224 warheads destroy
every Soviety city with a population
over 100,000.
But once I begin writing
the figures do not stop.
A 20 megaton

bomb, a firestorm rages over
3,000 acres.
A 1,000 megaton bomb
destroys
California
Nevada, Utah, Oregon,
Puget Sound.
Destroys.
California.

3
Thirty-seven days from my
fortieth birthday. I have
gone up and down this coast
so many times I could trace
the shape of it for you
with my hands, up
into the high cold trees, down
to warm water and
the sprawling city
where I was
born, 1943.
In that year
while I slept
not entirely wanted
in a still room
behind venetian blinds
somewhere in a foreign language
babies were set on fire.
Their cries did not wake me.
Only I breathed in the dust
of their deaths.

4
It is my love I hold back
hide
not wanting to be seen
scrawl of hand
writing
don't guess
don't guess at my
passion
a wholly wild and raging
love for this world.

5
(Home)
If you look in this block
in the North of California
you will find a house
perhaps a century old
with the original wood shingles
dark from years of sun
and fine old joints, the men

who made them are dead, the attic
made into a bedroom now, the
linoleum added in 1955.
Twenty years ago
I lived there, a student
studying the history of
Western Civilization, reading John Milton,
looking out the attic window
at a cement sidewalk
which was before just a
dirt path
and Spanish, and was before
perhaps, a forest or a
meadow, a field,
belonging to the Ohlone
who have all
even their children
even all traces of who they were
perished.

6

This is the world I was born into.
Very young I learned
my mother and my father
had a terrible sorrow.
And very young
I learned this sorrow from them.

7

The mind is vast
what we know small.
Do you think we are not all
sewn together?
I still argue with her
grit my teeth trying to feel
the pain that riddled her body
the day they told her
she would never walk.
I try to enter her mind
the night she took her own life.

Cells have memory!
I shout to her.
Science gave you
an unnecessary despair.

8

Nor do they argue
nor do they understand
nor do they know
but still it is so.
And there are structures of
unknowing
we call disbelief.

9

Every American city
with a population above
25,000
targeted.
A bomb with the
explosive power
of 20 million tons of TNT.
80 per cent of all cancers.
How is it,
this woman asks,
the brilliant efforts of
American scientists
have been put
to such destructive uses?

10

It is not real, they tell us,
this home we long for
but a dream of a place
that never
existed.
But it is so familiar!
And the longing in us is
ourselves.

11

This is the world I was born into.
I saw the wave and its white curl.
I saw branches coming from trees
like streams from rivers.
And the water poisoned
and the land.
I saw the whale leap out of the water
I saw my child's eyes come out of me
                         her first cry.
And the air, the rain acid.

Kyrie Eleison
Baruch atah
Hosana
Adonai
Do you love the world?

12

Suppose she lay down her bow.
And went into
that place
stepping so slowly
so surely

13

This is what I wanted to tell you.
This is what I wanted to say.
Words come late and dark

near sleep.
She said to me
my head was eating my heart.
And what is good?
What is bad?
The delicacy of transmission.
Old alliances fracture
like the cold branches of a
winter tree.
This is the closest I can get.
The world is washed in space.
It is the words she used
precisely those
and I could not remember them.
Only my conviction.
There was badness and goodness.
One was bad.
The other suffered.
And I wanted to
I wanted to mend her.
She told me the whole story
and I told her what was
good and what was bad,
and this was not what she needed.
You think I am trying
to throw away morality
but I am not.
I am not trying to
throw away caring.
In a dream
I see myself
a handsome man
walking without feeling
into a desert.
I am not like him
yet this dream comes to me
and I feel grief.
Out at the edge of this territory
is a missile.
I know for certain
this weapon is bad.
I do not try to mend her
and this makes me weep
for what she has suffered.

14
(The Enemy)
I wanted you to be good.
I wanted your judgements.
But all your rules became ash.
Your goodness was like an island.
(Your sainthood *was* the sin.)
Now that you have fallen

I cross the water
wrestle with you
charge you to bless me
watch as you
appear and disappear
become me.

15
The mind is vast.
A whale blows.
Shall we pitch ourselves into terror?
Shall we come home?
Enter darkness, weep
know the dimension
of absence, the unreachable deep.

16
How far can they go?
This is my speech
an American speech of whalers
and farmers what my
people did
plain, simple, honed
to the point
how far will they go?
Is there a stopping point?
Everyone knows there is not.

17
What can we make of this?
Two children held hostage together
in a van
for ten months.
What kind of man?
A girl, born three years ago
in California,
a boy who was born in
and survived Vietnam.
How far?
The children were continually beaten
with a rubber hose
and forced into sexual acts
in exchange for being fed.
I am a woman
who read this story
in a newspaper.

18
(Bone Cancer)
You must not let terror overtake you.
It is a bone breaking in the middle of the night.
It is a misspelled word.
It is everything you thought you knew
becoming unknown, the leaves
stripped from the tree,

all the greenness orange and dry,
it is pain past bearable, you must not.
Down the street in the darkness someone young
is dying. The soil, perhaps, under your feet
is poison, the water you drink.
What is this? Be reasonable. Disaster
is always predicted and look
we exist. Humanity had a day of birth,
slow, unreasoned, surprising. Now,
is it possible, is it possible
could this be?

19
Do we not want
this place
to find it
the body again
hearth, heart.
How is it I can say this
so that you will
see too what I have seen.
After the fires
(after the unspeakable)
there will be no home.
And what of us
will remain in memory?
Nothing?

20
At least we think of them.
The six million.
We long for them.
Want them to be like they were
before
want the music
their mothers and fathers sang
to pass from our lips.
And we ask
How is it they did not know?

21
Do you think it is right
to despair?
No, no, it is not about
right and wrong.
It is the thread
shining.

22
Kyrie Eleison
Baruch atah   adonai
Omne Padme
New rules
take the place of the old.
Be Here Now

is the lesson.
But I do not want to be.
I am one hundred years away
into the future.
My heart aches wondering.
Will this old tree grow even bigger?
Will its roots threaten the foundation of
                                        this house?
Will there be a daughter of a
        daughter of a daughter
        a son? And what is the
look in their eyes? Tell me
what you see there. And
do you like to watch
them as they walk across
fields.

Fields?

The sweet soul is sexual we say
lost in each other, what he called
the id is so much more and
no object in the universe travels faster
than the speed of light, we whisper,
love this motion of light
does not change, I see it
in the saying of it to you,
I hear in your hearing
your hands find me saying
yes, how everything
I could die, fits together,
and the sweet soul
is so large, so large, and hold
me so that bone bursts upon bone
and this is the bone of your face
I say astonished and let me be
possessed by astonishment
of you, your being and the history
of your bright speech breaking in me
as light on every distant feeling
the story of how you came here
evokes to fullness in me, taste
and take into your mouth, love, this sweetness
your sweetness you made in me
we say, shuddering, delight.

Marilyn Hacker

Eight Days in April

1
I broke a glass, got bloodstains on the sheet:
hereafter, must I only write you chaste
connubial poems? Now that I have traced
a way from there to here across the sweet-
est morning, rose-blushed blond, will measured feet
advance processionally, where before
they scuff-heeled flights of stairs, kicked at a door,
or danced in wing-tips to a dirty beat?
Or do I tell the world that I have got
rich quick, got lucky, (got laid,) got just what
the doctor ordered, more than I deserved?
This is the second morning I woke curved
around your dreaming. In one night, I've seen
moonset and sunrise in your lion's mane.

2
Moons set and suns rise in your lion's mane
through LP kisses or spread on my thighs.
Winter subsided while I fantasized
what April dawns frame in the windowpane.
Sweetheart, I'm still not getting enough sleep,
but I'm not tired, and outside it's spring
in which we sprang the afternoon shopping
after I'd been inside you, O so deep
I thought we would be tangled at the roots.
I think we are. (I've never made such noise.
I've never come so hard, or come so far
in such a short time.) You're an exemplar
piss-elegance is not reserved for boys.
Tonight we'll go out in our gangster suits.

3
Last night we went out in our gangster suits,
but just across the street to Santerello's,
waited past nine for wine. We shone; the fellows
noticed. "You have a splendid linen coat,"
Dimitri told you as he sat us down.
(This used to be my local; now it's chic.)
A restaurant table's like a bed: we speak
the way we do calmed after love, alone
in the dark. There's a lot to get to know.

We feel bad; we felt better. Soon I was
laid back enough to drink around the bend.
You got me home, to bed, like an old friend.
I like you, Robyn, when you're scared, because
you tough it out while you're feeling it through.

4

You tough it out while you're feeling it through,
but sometimes the bed's rocked over tidal waves
that aren't our pleasures. Everyone behaves
a little strangely when they're in a new
neighborhood, language, continent, time-zone.
We got here fast; your jet-lag's worse than mine.
I only had Paris to leave behind.
You left your whole young history. My own
reminds me to remind you, waking shaken
with tears, dream-racked, is standard for the course.
We need accommodation that allows
each one some storage space for her dead horse.
If the title weren't already taken,
I'd call this poem, "Directions to My House."

5

I'd call this poem, "Directions to My House,"
except today I'm writing it in yours,
in your paisley p.j's. The skylight pours
pale sunlight on white blankets. While I douse
my brain with coffee, you sleep on. Dream well
this time. We'll have three sets of keys apiece:
uptown, downtown, Paris on a sublease.
Teach me to drive. (Could I teach you to spell?)
I think the world's our house. I think I built
and furnished mine with space for you to move
through it, with me, alone in rooms, in love
with our work. I moved into one mansion
the morning when I touched, I saw, I felt
your face blazing above me like a sun.

6

Your face blazing above me like a sun-
deity, framed in red-gold flames, *gynandre*
in the travail of pleasure, urgent, tender
terrible—my epithalamion
circles that luminous intaglio
—and you under me as I take you there,
and you opening me in your mouth where
the waves inevitably overflow
restraint. No, no, that isn't the whole thing,
(also you drive like cop shows, and you sing
gravel and gold, are street-smart, book-smart,
laugh from your gut) but it is (a soothing
poultice applied to my afflicted part)
the central nervous system and the heart.

7
The central nervous system and the heart,
and whatever it is in me wakes me
at 5 AM regardless, and what takes me
(when you do) ineluctably apart
and puts me back together; the too-smart,
too-clumsy kid glutted on chocolate cakes (me
at ten); the left-brain righteousness that makes me
make of our doubled dailiness an art
are in your capable square hands. O sweet,
possessives make me antsy: we are free
to choose each other perpetually.
Though I don't think my French short-back-and-sides
means I'll be the most orthodox of brides,
I broke a glass, got bloodstains on the sheet.

Jessica Tarahata Hagedorn

Song for my Father

i arrive
in the unbearable heat
the sun's stillness
stretching across
the land's silence
people staring out
from airport cages
thousands of miles
later
and i have not yet understood
my obsession to return

and twelve years
is fast
inside my brain
exploding like tears

i could show you
but you already know.

you greet me
and i see
it is you
you all the time
pulling me back
towards this space

letters are the memory
i carry with me
the unspoken name
of you,
my father

in new york
they ask me if i'm puerto rican
and do i live in queens?

i listen to pop stations
chant to iemaja
convinced i'm really brazilian
and you a riverboat gambler
shooting dice in macao
during the war

roaches fly around us
like bats in twilight
and barry white grunts
in fashionable discotheques
setting the pace
for guerillas to grind

the president's wife
has a fondness for concert pianists
and gossip is integral
to conversation

if you eat enough papaya
your sex drive diminishes
lorenza paints my nails blue
and we giggle at the dinner table
aunts and whores
brothers and homosexuals
a contessa with chinese eyes
and an uncle cranky with loneliness
he carries an american passport
like me

and here we are,
cathedrals in our thighs
banana trees for breasts
and history all mixed up
saxophones in our voices
when we scream
the love of rhythms
inherent
when we dance

they can latin here
and shoot you
for the wrong glance
eyes that kill
eyes that kill

dope dealers are executed
in public
and senators go mad
in prison camps
the nightclubs are burning
with indifference
curfew drawing near
soldiers lurk in jeeps
of dawn warzones
as the president's daughter
boogies nostalgically
under the gaze
of sixteen smooth bodyguards
and decay is forever
even in the rage
of humorless revolutionaries

in hotel lobbies
we drink rum
testing each other's wit
snakes sometimes crawl
in our beds
but what can you do
in the heat
the laziness makes you love
so easily

you smile like buddha
from madrid
urging me to swim with you
the water is clear
with corpses
of dragonflies and
mosquitoes

i'm writing different poems now
my dreams have become reptilian
and green

everything green, green
and hot

eyes that kill
eyes that kill

women slither
in and out of barroom doorways
their tongues massage
the terror from your nightmares
the lizard hissing nervously
as he watches
you breathe

i am trapped
by overripe mangoes
i am trapped
by the beautiful sadness of women
i am trapped
by priests and nuns
whispering my name
in confession boxes
i am trapped
by antiques and the music
of the future

and leaving you
again and again
for america,
the loneliest of countries

my words change . . .
sometimes
i even forget english.

The Song of Bullets

Formalized
by middle age
we avoid crowds
but still
love music.

Day after day
with less surprise
we sit
in apartments
and count
the dead.

Awake,
my daughter croons
her sudden cries
and growls
my new language.
While she sleeps
we memorize
a list of casualties:

the photographer's brother
the doctor is missing.
Or I could say:
"Victor's brother Oscar
has been gone for two years. . . .
It's easier for the family
to think of him dead."

Victor sends
a Christmas card
from El Salvador:
"Things still the same."

And there are others
who don't play
by the rules—
someone else's brother
perhaps mine
languishes in a hospital;
everyone's grown tired
of his nightmares
and pretends
he's not there.

Someone else's father
perhaps mine
will be executed
when the time comes.
Someone else's mother
perhaps mine
telephones incessantly
her husband is absent

her son has gone mad
her lover has committed suicide
she's a survivor
who can't appreciate
herself.

The sight
of my daughter's
pink and luscious flesh
undoes me.
I fight
my weakening rage
I must remember
to commit
those names to memory
and stay angry.

Friends send postcards:
"Alternating between hectic
social Manila life & rural wonders
of Sagata . . . on to Hongkong and Bangkok—
Love . . ."

Assassins cruise the streets
in obtrusive limousines
sunbathers idle
on the beach

War is predicted
in five years
ten years
any day now
I always thought
it was already happening

snipers and poets locked
in a secret embrace
the country
my child may never see

a heritage
of women in heat
and men
skilled at betrayal

dancing
to the song
of bullets.

Joy Harjo

Bleed Through

I don't believe in promises, but there you are
balancing on a tightrope of sound.
You sneak into the world
inside a labyrinith of flame
break the walls beneath my ribs.
I yearn to sing; a certain note can spiral stars,
or knock the balance of the world askew.
Inside your horn lives a secret woman
who says she knows the power of the
womb,
can transform massacres into gold, her own heartache
into a ruby stone.
Her anger is yours and when her teeth bite through
a string of glass
you awaken, and it is not another dream
but your arms around a woman
who was once a dagger between your legs.
There are always ways to fall asleep,
but to be alive is to forsake
the fear of blood.
And dreams aren't excuses anymore. You are not behind
a smoking mirror,
but inside a ceremony of boulders that has survived
your many deaths.
It is not by accident you watch the sun
become your heart
sink into your belly then reappear in a town
that magnetically attracts you.
What attracts cannot naturally be separated.
A black hole reversed is a white hot star,
unravels this night
inside a song that is the same wailing cry as blue.
There are no words, only sounds
that lead us into the darkest nights,
where stars burn into ice
where the dead arise again
to walk in shoes of fire.

She Had Some Horses

She had some horses.

She had horses who were bodies of sand.
She had horses who were maps drawn of blood.
She had horses who were skins of ocean water.
She had horses who were the blue air of sky.
She had horses who were fur and teeth.
She had horses who were clay and would break.
She had horses who were splintered red cliff.

She had some horses.

She had horses with long, pointed breasts.
She had horses with full, brown thighs.
She had horses who laughed too much.
She had horses who threw rocks at glass houses.
She had horses who licked razor blades.

She had some horses.

She had horses who danced in their mother's arms.
She had horses who thought they were the sun and their
bodies shone and burned like stars.
She had horses who waltzed nightly on the moon.
She had horses who were much too shy, and kept quiet
in stalls of their own making.

She had some horses.

She had horses who liked Creek Stomp Dance songs.
She had horses who cried in their beer.
She had horses who spit at male queens who made
them afraid of themselves.
She had horses who said they weren't afraid.
She had horses who lied.
She had horses who told the truth, who were stripped
bare of their tongues.

She had some horses.

She had horses who called themselves, "horse".
She had horses who called themselves, "spirit", and kept
their voices secret and to themselves.
She had horses who had no names.
She had horses who had books of names.

She had some horses.

She had horses who whispered in the dark, who were afraid to
speak.
She had horses who screamed out of fear of the silence, who
carried knives to protect themselves from ghosts.
She had horses who waited for destruction.
She had horses who waited for resurrection.

She had some horses.

She had horses who got down on their knees for any savior.
She had horses who thought their high price had saved them.
She had horses who tried to save her, who climbed in her
bed at night and prayed as they raped her.

She had some horses.

She had some horses she loved.
She had some horses she hated.

These were the same horses.

Nine Below

Across the frozen Bering Sea is the invisible border
of two warring countries. I am loyal to neither,

only to the birds who fly over, laugh at the ridiculous
ways of humans, know wars destroy dreams, divide the

country, inside us. Last night there was a breaking
wave, in the center of a dream war. You were there, but

I couldn't see you. Woke up cold in a hot house. Didn't
sleep but fought the distances I had imagined, and went

back to find you. I called my heart's dogs, gave them
the sound of your blue saxophone to know you by, and let

them smell the shirt you wore when we last made love.
I walked with them south along the white sea, and

crossed to the fiery plane of my dreaming. We circled
the place; you weren't there. I found nothing I could see,

no trace of war, of you, but the dogs barked, rolled
in your smell, ears pricked at what they could hear that

I couldn't. They ran to me, licked the smell of the wet
tracks of your mouth from my neck, my shoulder. They

smelled your come on my fingers, my face. They felt the
quivering nerve of emotion that forced me to live. It

made them nervous, excited. I loosened my mind's rein;
let them find you.

I watched them follow the invisible connection. They
traveled a spiral arc through an Asiatic burst of time.

There were no false boundaries between countries, between
us. They climbed the polar ice, saw it melt.

They flew through the shimmering houses of the gods,
crossed over into your childhood, and then south.

When they arrived in your heart's atmosphere it was
an easy sixty degrees. The war was over, it had never

begun, and you were alive and laughing, standing beneath
a fat sun, calling me home.

Resurrection

Estelí
       this mountain town means something
                  like the glass of bloody stars.
Your Spanish tongue will not be silent.
                      In my volcano heart,
soldiers pace, watch over what they fear.
                One pretty one leans against
                      his girlfriend
they make promises, touch, plan to meet somewhere else
                      in this war.
Not far down the fevered street
            a trace of calypso
                laughter from a cantina.
We are all in a balloon that's about to split.
              Candles make oblique circles
in the barrio church, line the walls with prayers.
                An aboriginal woman
as old as Momotombo fingers obsidian
            recalls dreams, waits for the light
to begin to break. I don't imagine anything.
            Lizards chase themselves all night
over the tin roof of the motel.
              I rock in a barrage of fever,
feel the breathing-sweat of the whole town: stop, pause
                and begin again.
I have no damned words to make violence fit neatly
              like wrapped packages
of meat, to hold us safely.
         The songs here speak tenderly of honor and love,
sweet melody is the undercurrent of gunfire,
                yet
the wounded and the dead call out in words that sting
           like bitter limes. Ask the women
who have given away the clothes of their dead children. Ask the
                frozen
soul of a man who was found buried in the hole left
           by his missing penis.
They are talking, yet
        the night could change.
We all watch for fire
        for all the fallen dead to return

and teach us a language so terrible
                              it could resurrect us all.

Mercy

Mercy
      on this morning where in the air is a flash
of what could be the salvation of spring.
                              After all this winter
I mean, it wasn't just devil snow that rode us hard.
Mail me to Jamaica.
                  I want to lay out on steaming beaches.
Find my way back through glacier ice another way.
Forget the massacres, proclamations of war,
                              rumors of war.
I won't pour rifle shot through the guts of someone
I'm told is my enemy.
                  Hell, my own enemy is right here.
Can you look inside, see past the teeth worn down
by meat and anger,
                  can you see?
                              Sometimes the only filter
is a dead cat in the road.
                  Sucks your belly up to your teeth
in fear of what might happen to you,
                              all your sins
chase you in the street
                  string what you thought was the only you
into a greasy field. Then you could get scared
                              decide to run away
wear a uniform, get to shooting at someone who looks just like
                                          you
                  so you can be free to enter the next world,
looks like Las Vegas, filled with food, wine
                              and the finest women.
Safe, so safe, like a beach in Jamaica
                  where the blood stains have already
soaked through to the bottom of the Caribbean
            so you don't have to see
                              unless this flash
becomes a bayonet of sound, hands of fire
to lead you to yourself
                  til you cry
                        mercy.

The Woman Hanging from the Thirteenth Floor Window

She is the woman hanging from the 13th floor
window. Her hands are pressed white against the
concrete moulding of the tenement building. She
hangs from the 13th floor window in east Chicago,
with a swirl of birds over her head. They could
be a halo, or a storm of glass waiting to crush her.

She thinks she will be set free.

The woman hanging from the 13th floor window
on the east side of Chicago is not alone.
She is a woman of children, of the baby, Carlos,
and of Margaret, and of Jimmy who is the oldest.
She is her mother's daughter and her father's son.
She is several pieces between the two husbands
she has had. She is all the women of the apartment
building who stand watching her, watching themselves.

When she was young she ate wild rice on scraped down
plates in warm wood rooms. It was in the farther
north and she was the baby then. They rocked her.

She sees Lake Michigan lapping at the shores of
herself. It is a dizzy hole of water and the rich
live in tall glass houses at the edge of it. In some
places Lake Michigan speaks softly, here, it just sputters
and butts itself against the asphalt. She sees
other buildings just like hers. She sees other
women hanging from many-floored windows
counting their lives in the palms of their hands
and in the palms of their children's hands.

She is the woman hanging from the 13th floor window
on the Indian side of town. Her belly is soft from
her children's births, her worn levis swing down below
her waist, and then her feet, and then her heart.
She is dangling.

The woman hanging from the 13th floor hears voices.
They come to her in the night when the lights have gone
dim. Sometimes they are little cats mewing and scratching
at the door, sometimes they are her grandmother's voice,
and sometimes they are gigantic men of light whispering
to her to get up, to get up, to get up. That's when she wants
to have another child to hold onto in the night, to be able
to fall back into dreams.

And the woman hanging from the 13th floor window
hears other voices. Some of them scream out from below
for her to jump, they would push her over. Others cry softly
from the sidewalks, pull their children up like flowers and gather
them into their arms. They would help her, like themselves.

But she is the woman hanging from the 13th floor window,
and she knows she is hanging by her own fingers, her
own skin, her own thread of indecision.

She thinks of Carlos, of Margaret, of Jimmy.
She thinks of her father, and of her mother.
She thinks of all the women she has been, of all
the men. She thinks of the color of her skin, and
of Chicago streets, and of waterfalls and pines.
She thinks of moonlight nights, and of cool spring storms.
Her mind chatters like neon and northside bars.
She thinks of the 4 a.m. lonelinesses that have folded
her up like death, discordant, without logical and
beautiful conclusion. Her teeth break off at the edges.
She would speak.

The woman hangs from the 13th floor window crying for
the lost beauty of her own life. She sees the
sun falling west over the grey plane of Chicago.
She thinks she remembers listening to her own life
break loose, as she falls from the 13th floor
window on the east side of Chicago, or as she
climbs back up to claim herself again.

Linda Hogan

The Other Side

At sunset
the white horse has disappeared
over the edge of earth
like the sun running from the teeth of darkness.

Fleeing past men who clean weapons
in sudden light, women
breaking eggs in faith
that new ones will grow
radiant in feather cribs
the coyotes watch over.

All the innocent predators!
Even the moon can't stop to rest
in the tree's broken arm,
and at sunset the cows of the field turn away
from the world
wearing a death mask.

White horse.
White horse
I listen for you to return
like morning
from the open mouth of the underworld,
kicking in its teeth.
I listen for the sound of you
tamping fast earth, a testimony
of good luck nailed to hooves.

Even the moon can't stop to rest,
and the broken branch is innocent
of its own death
as it goes on breathing
what's in the air these days
radiating soft new leaves,
telling a story about the other side of creation.

The New Apartment, Minneapolis

The floorboards creak.
The moon is on the wrong side of the building,

and burns remain
on the floor.

The house wants to fall down
the universe when earth turns.

It still holds the coughs of old men
and their canes tapping on the floor.

I think of Indian people here before me
and how last spring white merchants hung an elder

on a meathook and beat him;
he was one of The People.

I remember this war
and all the wars

and relocation like putting the moon in prison
with no food and that moon was a crescent

but be warned, the moon grows full again
and the roofs of this town are all red

and we are looking through the walls of houses
at people suspended in air.

Some are baking, with flour on their hands,
or sleeping on floor three, or getting drunk.

I see the business men who hit their wives
and the men who are tender fathers.

There are women crying or making jokes.
Children are laughing under beds.

Girls in navy blue robes talk on the phone all night
and some Pawnee is singing 49's, drumming the table.

Inside the walls
world changes are planned, bosses overthrown.

If we had no coffee,
cigarettes or liquor,

says the woman in room 12,
they'd have a revolution on their hands.

Beyond walls are lakes and plains,
canyons and the universe;

the stars are the key
turning in the lock of night.

Turn the deadbolt and I am home.
I have walked to the dark earth,

opened a door to nights where there are no apartments,
just drumming and singing;

The Duck Song, The Snake Song,
The Drunk Song.

No one here remembers the city
or has ever lost the will to go on.

Hello aunt, hello brothers, hello trees
and deer walking quietly on the soft red earth.

To Light

At the spring
we hear the great seas traveling
underground
giving themselves up
with tongues of water
that sing the earth open.

They have journeyed through the graveyards
of our loved ones,
turning in their graves
to carry the stories of life to air.

Even the trees with their rings
have kept track
of the crimes that live within
and against us.

We remember it all.
We remember, though we are just skeletons
whose organs and flesh
hold us in.
We have stories
as old as the great seas
breaking through the chest
flying out the mouth,
noisy tongues that once were silenced,
all the ocenas we contain
coming to light.

Seeing Through the Sun

How dishonest the sun,
making ruined cities
look like dust.

In that country of light
there is no supper
though the sun's market place
reveals the legs inside young women's skirts,
burning round oranges,
wheat loaves,
and the men's uniforms with shining buttons.

We are polite in the sun
and we ask for nothing
because it has hit the walls with such force.

But when the sun falls
and we are all one color
and still in danger
we tell each other
how this child was broken open by a man,
this person left with only fingerprints.

Sometimes one of us
tries to stand up to the light.
Her skin burns red as a liar
in fear's heat.
So in the light we say only,
Never mind, I was just passing through
the universe. It's nothing.

But there are times we tell the truth;
Sun, we see through you
the flashing of rifles and scythes.

Let's stand up. The enemy
is ready for questions.
There is light coming in beneath the door.
Stop it with a rag.
There is light entering a keyhole.
Cover it with your hand
and speak, tell me everything.

June Jordan

Getting Down to Get Over

dedicated to my mother

MOMMA MOMMA MOMMA
momma momma
mammy
nanny
granny
woman
mistress
sista

luv

blackgirl
slavegirl

gal

honeychile
sweetstuff
sugar
sweetheart
baby
Baby baby

MOMMA MOMMA
Black Momma
Black bitch
Black pussy
piecea tail
nice piecea ass

hey daddy! hey
bro!
we walk together (an')
talk together (an')
dance and *do*
(together)
dance and do/hey!
daddy!
bro!
hey!
nina nikki nonni nommo nommo

momma Black
Momma

Black Woman
Black
Female Head of Household
Black Matriarchal Matriarchy
Black Statistical
Lowlife Lowlevel Lowdown
Lowdown and *up*
to be Low-down
Black Statistical
Low Factor
Factotem
Factitious Fictitious
Figment Figuring in Lowdown Lyin
Annual Reports

Black Woman/Black
Hallelujah Saintly
patient
smilin
humble
givin thanks
for
Annual Reports and
Monthly Dole
and
Friday night
and
(*good* God!)
Monday mornin: Black and Female
martyr masochist
(A BIG WHITE LIE)
Momma Momma

What does Mothafuckin mean?
WHO'S THE MOTHAFUCKA
FUCKED MY MOMMA
messed yours over
and right now
be trippin on my starveblack
female soul
a macktruck
mothafuck
the first primordial
the paradig/digmatic
dogmatistic mothafucka who
is he?
hey!
momma momma

dry eyes on the
shy/dark/hidden/cryin Black
face

108

of the loneliness
the rape
the brokeup mailbox
an' no western union roses
come inside the kitchen
and no poem
take you through the whole night
and no big
Black
burly
hand
he holdin yours
to have to hold onto
no
big Black burly hand
no nommo
no Black prince
come riding from the darkness
on a beautiful black horse
no bro
no daddy

"I was sixteen when I met my father.
In a bar.
In Baltimore.
He told me who he was
and what he does.
Paid for the drinks.
I looked.
I listened.
And I left him.
It was civil
perfectly
and absolute bull
shit.
The drinks was leakin waterweak
and never got down to my knees."

hey daddy
what they been and done to you
and what you been and done
to me
to momma
momma momma
hey
sugar daddy
big daddy
sweet daddy
Black Daddy
The Original Father Divine
the everlovin
deep
tall
bad

buck
jive
cold
strut
bop
split
tight
loose
close
hot
hot
hot
sweet SWEET DADDY
WHERE YOU BEEN AND
WHEN YOU COMIN BACK TO ME
HEY
WHEN YOU COMIN BACK
TO MOMMA
momma momma

And Suppose He Finally Say
"Look, Baby.
I Loves Me Some
Everything about You.
Let Me Be Your Man."
That reach around the hurtin
like a dream.
And I ain never wakin up
from that one.
momma momma
momma momma

II
Consider the Queen

hand on her hip
sweat restin from
the corn/bean/greens' field
steamy under the pale/sly
suffocatin sun

Consider the Queen

she fix the cufflinks
on his Sunday shirt
and fry some chicken
bake some cake
and tell the family
"Never mine about the bossman
don' know how a human
bein spozed to act. Jus'
never mind about him.
Wash your face.
Sit down. And let
the good Lord bless this table."

Consider the Queen

her babies pullin at the nipples
pullin at the momma milk

the infant fingers gingerly
approach caress the
soft/Black/swollen/momma breast

and there
inside the mommasoft
life-spillin treasure chest
the heart
breaks

rage by grief by sorrow
weary weary
breaks
breaks quiet
silently
the weary sorrow
quiet now the furious
the adamant the broken
busted beaten down and beaten up
the beaten beaten beaten
weary heart beats
tender-steady
and the babies suck/
the seed of blood
and love glows at the
soft/Black/swollen momma breast

Consider the Queen

she works when she works
in the laundry *in jail*
in the school house *in jail*
in the office *in jail*
on the soap box *in jail*
on the desk
on the floor
on the street
on the line
at the door
lookin fine
at the head of the line
steppin sharp from behind
in the light
with a song
wearing boots
or a belt
and a gun
drinkin wine when it's time
when the long week is done
but she works when she works

111

in the laundry in jail
she works when she works

Consider the Queen

she sleeps when she sleeps
with the king in the kingdom
she
sleeps when she sleeps
with the wall
with whatever it is who happens
to call
with me and with you
(to survive you make
do/you explore more and more)
so she sleeps when she sleeps
a really deep sleep

Consider the Queen

a full/Black/glorious/a purple rose
aroused by the tiger breathin
beside her
a shell with the moanin
of ages inside her
a hungry one feedin the folk
what they need

Consider the Queen.

III
Blackman
let that white girl go
she know what you ought to know.
(By now.)

IV
MOMMA MOMMA
momma momma
family face
face of the family alive
momma
mammy
momma
woman
sista
baby
luv

the house on fire/
poison waters/
earthquake/
and the air a nightmare/
turn
turn
turn around the
national gross product

growin
really gross/turn
turn
turn the pestilence away
the miserable killers
and Canarsie
Alabama
people beggin to be people
warfare on the welfare
of the folk/
hey
turn
turn away
the trickbag university/the
trickbag propaganda/
trickbag
tricklins of prosperity/of
pseudo-"status"
lynchtree necklace
on the strong
round
neck of you
my momma
momma momma
turn away
the f.b.i./the state police/the cops/
the/everyone of the
infest/incestuous investigators
into you
and Daddy/into us
hey
turn
my mother
turn
the face of history
to your own
and please be smilin
if you can
be smilin
at the family

momma momma

let the funky forecast
be the last
one we will ever
want to listen to

And Daddy see
the stars fall down
and burn a light
into the singin
darkness of your eyes
my Daddy

my blackman
you take my body in
your arms/you use
the oil of coconuts/of trees and
flowers/fish and new fruits
from the new world
to enflame me in this otherwise
cold place
please
meanwhile
momma
momma momma
teach me how to kiss
the king within the kingdom
teach me how to t.c.b./to make do
and be
like you
teach me to survive my
momma
teach me how to hold a new life
momma
help me
turn the face of history
to your face.

Faye Kicknosway

Lament:

And what shall I be today, what
shall I be today? Oh, my wheat hair,
my crayon eyes, my fingers more strong
than nylon rope; what
shall I be today?

And when I've used my dreaming up,
when it's gone, when winter moves
across my hair, and my eyes fade
like old paper, and my fingers crack
and claw; oh,

what shall I have left that day
to keep me whole and warm?
What dream will I have left that day
if they're all gone?

Gracie, 1967

You're a hillbilly and you come to a place like Detroit,
a place bigger than any place you've ever been.
All you can do is pass coffee over a counter.
A dark, foreign man comes along and asks you to marry him.
You go home,

dressed alright and wearing nice jewelry.
You park the car at the foot of the road
because it's springtime
and you walk up the hill to the house.
Ma sticks her hand out the window,
waving,
until she sees how dark he is.
What does she know, how far past the chicken coop
did she ever go?
How many men in the bushes
and in cars at the side of the road
with their mouths and their zippers,

how far past the chicken coop did she ever go,
telling me,

"Didn't I raise you better?"
She thinks it's easy
living up here?
Men're falling over themselves to marry me,
what I do,
because that's what they're thinking
when they look at me:
what I do.
No man is going to kill himself hauling me off
to a preacher.
What does she know, always around the house,
never farther than the chicken yard, except maybe to church,
sometimes down the road wearing a bonnet?
How can she say she raised me better?
Better than what?
I'm supposed to spend my life feeding the chickens?
Better than what?

What does she know?
So he's dark and short and talks funny;
no other man asked me to marry him,
no other man put his hands on me like I'm special.
I'm supposed to look at how dark he is
and listen to how funny he talks
and tell him to go when he asks me to marry him?

I go home with my husband,
to introduce him to my folks,
and my daddy comes around the side of the house,
and my two brothers stand on the porch
with their hands tucked into their pants,
and my ma stops waving
"howdy do; welcome",
and points her finger at him,
at my husband,
and says,
"What're you bringing home, Sister?
What're you bringing home?"

from Night Braid

6
I am the woman of sweaty language, the belly
woman, the thigh woman.
I am the dunce, the maker of deliberate
magic, the obedient, the harmed.

I make the sky
perfect.
I put the stars in their sockets.

Loving him is whist and aspirin.
There is no country to it
nor city
nor anything held long enough
for a good look.

I want to hear
the metaphor of a porch swing, its wood,
the house creaking, lovers broken open,
visible.

I want this air
this dreamless air
let loose.

He limits me;
I am a pet: sit, beg.
He tells me I'm kind of nice
to have around.

He is the season of lilac.
Disease.

He sleeps.
I stand up, full of teeth,
scorned,
put aside.

My hair is white with anger.
There is fire in my legs.

I am dark,
the woman of gypsy people, the beggar,
fortune teller.
I am a gesture of hands, voice.
He lies with me
because I invite it,
I speak it.

I will not be ashen.
I will not be stitched
in the seam of an outside pocket.

Let him limit his cat,
his coat hangers,
the size of his footprints.
Let him limit dust.

Carolyn Kizer

The Intruder

My mother—preferring the strange to the tame:
Dove-note, bone marrow, deer dung,
Frog's belly distended with finny young,
Leaf-mould wilderness, hare-bell, toadstool,
Odd, small snakes roving through the leaves,
Metallic beetles rambling over stones: all
Wild and natural!—flashed out her instinctive love, and quick, she
Picked up the fluttering, bleeding bat the cat laid at her feet,
And held the little horror to the mirror, where
He gazed on himself, and shrieked like an old screen door far off.

Depended from her pinched thumb, each wing
Came clattering down like a small black shutter.
Still tranquil, she began, "It's rather sweet. . . ."
The soft mouse body, the hard feral glint
In the caught eyes. Then we saw,
And recoiled: lice, pallid, yellow,
Nested within the wing-pits, cosily sucked and snoozed.
The thing dropped from her hands, and with its thud,
Swiftly, the cat, with a clean careful mouth
Closed on the soiled webs, growling, took them out to the back
                                              stoop.

But still, dark blood, a sticky puddle on the floor
Remained, of all my mother's tender, wounding passion
For a whole wild, lost, betrayed and secret life
Among its dens and burrows, its clean stones,
Whose denizens can turn upon the world
With spitting tongue, an odor, talon, claw,
To sting or soil benevolence, alien
As our clumsy traps, our random scatter of shot.
She swept to the kitchen. Turning on the tap,
She washed and washed the pity from her hands.

A Widow in Wintertime

Last night a baby gargled in the throes
Of a fatal spasm. My children are all grown
Past infant strangles; so, reassured, I knew
Some other baby perished in the snow.
But no. The cat was making love again.

Later, I went down and let her in.
She hung her tail, flagging from her sins.
Though she'd eaten, I forked out another dinner,
Being myself hungry all ways, and thin
From metaphysic famines she knows nothing of,

The feckless beast! Even so, resemblances
Were on my mind: female and feline, though
She preens herself from satisfaction, and does
Not mind lying even in snow. She is
Lofty and bedraggled, without need to choose.

As an ex-animal, I look fondly on
her excesses and simplicities, and would not return
To them; taking no marks for what I have become,
Merely that my nine lives peal in my ears again
And again, ring in these austerities,

These arbitrary disciplines of mine,
Most of them trivial: like covering
The children on my way to bed, and trying
To live well enough alone, and not to dream
Of grappling in the snow, claws plunged in fur,

Or waken in a caterwaul of dying.

Thrall

The room is sparsely furnished:
A chair, a table and a father.

He sits in the chair by the window.
There are books on the table.
The time is always just past lunch.

You tiptoe past as he eats his apple
And reads. He looks up, angry.
He has heard your asthmatic breathing.

He will read for years without looking up
Until your childhood is over:

Smells, untidiness and boring questions;
Blood, from the first skinned knees

To the first stained thighs;
The foolish tears of adolescent love.

One day he looks up, pleased
At the finished product.
Now he is ready to love you!

So he coaxes you in the voice reserved
For reading Keats. You agree to everything.

Drilled in silence and duty,
You will give him no cause for reproach.
He will boast of you to strangers.

When the afternoon is older
Shadows in a smaller room
Fall on the bed, the books, the father.

You read aloud to him
"La Belle Dame sans Merci."
You feed him his medicine.
You tell him you love him.

You wait for his eyes to close at last
So you may write this poem.

Irena Klepfisz

Dedication from Bashert★

These words are dedicated to those who died
These words are dedicated to those who died
because they had no love and felt alone in the world
because they were afraid to be alone and tried to stick it out
because they could not ask
because they were shunned
because they were sick and their bodies could not resist the
disease
because they played it safe
because they had no connections
because they had no faith
because they felt they did not belong and wanted to die

These words are dedicated to those who died
because they were loners and liked it
because they acquired friends and drew others to them
because they took risks
because they were stubborn and refused to give up
because they asked for too much

These words are dedicated to those who died
because a card was lost and a number was skipped
because a bed was denied
because a place was filled and no other place was left

These words are dedicated to those who died
because someone did not follow through
because someone was overworked and forgot
because someone left everything to God
because someone was late
because someone did not arrive at all
because someone told them to wait and they just couldn't any
longer

These words are dedicated to those who died
because death is a punishment
because death is a reward
because death is the final rest
because death is eternal rage

These words are dedicated to those who died

Bashert

★*ba-shert* (Yiddish): inevitable, (pre)destined.

These words are dedicated to those who survived
These words are dedicated to those who survived
because their second grade teacher gave them books
because they did not draw attention to themselves and got lost
in the shuffle
because they knew someone who knew someone else who could
help them and bumped into them on a corner on a Thursday
afternoon
because they played it safe
because they were lucky

These words are dedicated to those who survived
because they knew how to cut corners
because they drew attention to themselves and always got picked
because they took risks
because they had no principles and were hard

These words are dedicated to those who survived
because they refused to give up and defied statistics
because they had faith and trusted in God
because they expected the worst and were always prepared
because they were angry
because they could ask
because they mooched off others and saved their strength
because they endured humiliation
because they turned the other cheek
because they looked the other way

These words are dedicated to those who survived
because life is a wilderness and they were savage
because life is an awakening and they were alert
because life is a flowering and they blossomed
because life is a struggle and they struggled
because life is a gift and they were free to accept it

These words are dedicated to those who survived

Bashert

Etlekhe verter oyf mame-loshn/
A few words in the mother tongue

lemoshl: for example

di kurve the whore
a woman who acknowledges her passions

di yidene the Jewess the Jewish woman
ignorant overbearing
let's face it: every woman is one

122

di yente the gossip the busybody
who knows what's what
and is never caught off guard

di lezbianke the one with
a roommate though we never used
the word

dos vaybl the wife
or the little woman

  ★ ★ ★

in der heym at home
where she does everything to keep
yidishkayt alive

yidishkayt a way of being
Jewish always arguable

in mark where she buys
di kartofl un khalah
(yes, potatoes and challah)

di kartofl the physical counter-
part of *yidishkayt*

mit tsibeles with onions
that bring *trern tsu di oygn*
tears to her eyes when she sees
how little it all is
veyniker un veyniker
less and less

di khalah braided
vi irh hor far der khasene
like her hair before the wedding
when she was *aza sheyn meydl*
such a pretty girl

di lange shvartse hor
the long black hair
di lange shvartse hor

  ★ ★ ★

a froy kholmt a woman
dreams *ihr ort oyf der velt*
her place in this world
un zi hot moyre and she is afraid
so afraid of the words
kurve
yidene
yente
lezbianke
vaybl

zi kholmt she dreams
un zi hot moyre and she is afraid

123

ihr ort
di velt
di heym
der mark

a meydl kholmt
a kurve kholmt
a yidene kholmt
a yente kholmt
a lezbianke kholmt

a vaybl kholmt
di kartofl
di khalah

yidishkayt

zi kholmt
di hor
di lange shvartse hor

zi kholmt
zi kholmt
zi kholmt

Royal Pearl

Where do new varieties come from?
General Eisenhower is a red tulip which was first recognized in 1951.
In 1957 a lemon yellow mutation appeared in a field of red General
Eisenhower tulips. This yellow mutation proved to be a stable sport
which was called—Royal Pearl.

—Brooklyn Botanic Gardens

In dead of winter   imprisoned within
the imprisoned earth   it was a leap
defiant   of all eternal laws   and patterns.
Beneath the frozen earth   it came to be
like a splitting of an inner will
a wrenching from a designated path
a sudden burst   from a cause unknown.
And then in spring   it opened: a lemon yellow
in a pure red field.

Our words deny the simple beauty
the wild energy of the event. *Anomaly*
deviant   mutant   we're always taught
as though this world   were a finished place
and we the dull guardians   of its perfected forms.
Our lives are rooted in such words.

Yet each winter   there are some

who watch   the gardens   emptied
only white   as the snow presses
on the fenced-in grounds   just
as on an unclaimed field.
And each winter   there are some
who dream   of a splitting of an inner will
a wrenching from the designated path
who dream a purple flower   standing solitary
in a yellow field.

Maxine Kumin

Shopping in Ferney with Voltaire

Wearing a flowered nightgown
under his frockcoat, Voltaire
comes down the avenue of oaks
a basket on his arm. Looks
four ways at his poète-philosophe
likeness in the square
that vélomoteurs dive toward
careening off to either side
and walks into the crowd
of tidy Genevoises who swarm
each Saturday across the line
to stroll along the cobblestones
choosing among a hundred cheeses
sandbagged sausages
dripping Breton artichokes
oysters, olives, almonds, dates.

A little chitchat seems appropriate.
I ask him how he feels.
Fingering the fringy cornucopias
of black chanterelles
(les trompettes de la mort) he quotes
himself: qui veut voir une ombre?
I've read that in the Besterman
biography. Also about
the colic on demand.
Also the fainting fits
to dispatch hangers-on.

We rummage among the burly roots
fresh dug from local plots.
He chooses small white turnips
to tuck around the Sunday roast.
I tell him his remains
were exhumed thirteen years post-mortem.
Someone stole two teeth and his left foot.
He shrugs.—A useless passion,
necrophilia. About
that stupid recantation:
remember that I never took
communion! Let's be clear on that.
I told the Abbé, you will note

I'm spitting blood.
We must be careful not
to mingle mine with God's.
He grins. We stop at carts of citrus fruits
collect a dozen clementines
and pay with clanks of old-style coins.

One booth away
Amnesty International
has prisoners for sale.
Handbills cry aloud
the murdered, the disappeared,
the tortured, in before-
and-after photographs.
A self-improvement course
run riot in reverse.
Anyone who cares to can
adopt a prisoner of conscience.
Voltaire's list is longer than
old-school homework Latin scansions.

In my day—he sighs
reliving the stench of pain
—torture was a public act.
Before they killed a man
they broke him on the rack.
The main thing was to die
courageously. It's different now.
No longer personal.
His sharp fox face so like
Max Adrian's Pangloss
as if he had just caught
out of the corner of his eye
the murderings en masse.
The nuclear juggernaut.
The Great Beast lumbering past.
The labor camps, the stripping off
of civilization's mask.

We walk together toward
the border at Meyrin.
The sky goes yellow as
old corn shucks. Rain will drench
the ancient hills, thorn-fenced,
these stubbled fields, the cows
kneeling along the ridge.
Behind us, Ferney brims with light.
—Adieu, he says.—Take my advice.
Always live close to the edge
so that when sudden flight
is called for, you can put
a foot down on the other side.
We embrace three times, à la suisse.
I cross the *douane*, then turn

to watch the old philosopher
mushrooms, roots, and tangerines in hand
limp back to the Enlightenment
and disappear.

Our Ground Time Here Will Be Brief

Blue landing lights make
nail holes in the dark.
A fine snow falls. We sit
on the tarmac taking on
the mail, quick freight,
trays of laboratory mice,
coffee and Danish for
the passengers.

Wherever we're going
is Monday morning.
Wherever we're coming from
is Mother's lap.
On the cloud-pack above, strewn
as loosely as parsnip
or celery seeds, lie
the souls of the unborn:

my children's children's
children and their father.
We gather seed for the last run
and lift off into the weather.

Relearning the Language of April

Where this man walks his fences
the willows do pliés with green laces,
eyelashes fly from the white plums,
the gaunt elms begin to open their frames.

When he passes, lithe with morning,
the terriers, rump-deep in a chuckhole,
boom out to follow,
the squirrels chirrup like cardinals.

Five prick-eared ponies
lift from their serious chewing.

The doomed cattle, wearing
intelligent smiles, turn.

For miles around, the plowed fields
release a sweet rancidness
warm as sperm.

I lie in the fat lap of noon
overhearing the doves' complaint.
Far off, a stutter of geese raise alarms.

Once more, body, Old Paint,
how could you trick me like this
in spring's blowzy arms?

Changing the Children

Anger does this.
Wishing the furious wish
turns the son into a crow,
the daughter, a porcupine.

Soon enough, no matter how
we want them to be happy
our little loved ones, no
matter how we prod them
into our sun that it may
shine on them, they whine
to stand in the dry-goods store.
Fury slams in.
The willful fury befalls.

Now the varnish-black son in a tree
crow the berater, denounces the race
of fathers, and the golden daughter
all arched bristle and quill
leaves scribbles on the tree bark
writing how The Nameless One
accosted her in the dark.

How put an end to this cruel spell?
Drop the son from the tree with a rifle.
Introduce maggots under his feathers
to eat down to the pure bone of boy.

In spring when the procupine comes
all stealth and waddle to feed on the willows
stun her with one blow of the sledge
and the entrapped girl will fly out
crying Daddy! or Danny!
or is it Darling?

And we will live all in bliss
for a year and a day until
the legitimate rage of parents
speeds the lad off this time
in the uniform of a toad
who spews a contagion of warts
while the girl contracts to a spider
forced to spin from her midseam
the saliva of false repentance.

Eventually we get them back.
Now they are grown up.
They are much like ourselves.
They wake mornings beyond cure,
not a virgin among them.
We are civil to one another.
We stand in the kitchen
slicing bread, drying spoons,
and tuning in to the weather.

Making the Jam Without You
for Judy

Old daughter, small traveler
asleep in a German featherbed
under the eaves in a postcard town
of turrets and towers,
I am putting a dream in your head.

Listen! Here it is afternoon.
The rain comes down like bullets.
I stand in the kitchen,
that harem of good smells
where we have bumped hips and
cracked the cupboards with our talk
while the stove top danced with pots
and it was not clear who did
the mothering. Now I am
crushing blackberries
to make the annual jam
in a white cocoon of steam.

Take it, my sleeper. Redo it
in any of your three
languages and nineteen years.
Change the geography.
Let there be a mountain,
the fat cows on it belled
like a cathedral. Let

there be someone beside you
as you come upon the ruins
of a schloss, all overgrown
with a glorious thicket,
its brambles soft as wool.
Let him bring the buckets
crooked on his angel arms
and may the berries, vaster
than any forage in
the mild hills of New Hampshire,
drop in your pail, plum size,
heavy as the eyes
of any honest dog
and may you bear them
home together to a square
white unreconstructed kitchen
not unlike this one.

Now may your two heads
touch over the kettle,
over the blood of the berries
that drink up sugar and sun,
over that tar-thick boil
love cannot stir down.
More plainly than
the bric-a-brac of shelves
filling with jelly glasses,
more surely than
the light driving through them
trite as rubies, I see him
as pale as paraffin beside you.
I see you cutting
fresh baked bread to spread it
with the bright royal fur.

At this time
I lift the flap of your dream
and slip out thinner than a sliver
as your two mouths open
for the sweet stain of purple.

Grandchild

for Yann

All night the *douanier* in his sentry box
at the end of the lane where France begins plays fox
and hounds with little spurts of cars
that sniff to a stop at the barrier

and declare themselves. I stand at the window
watching the ancient boundaries that flow
between my daughter's life and mine dissolve
like taffy pulled until it melts in half
without announcing any point of strain
and I am a young unsure mother again
stiffly clutching the twelve-limbed raw
creature that broke from between my legs, that stew
of bone membrane loosely sewn up in
a fierce scared flailing other being.

We blink, two strangers in a foreign kitchen.
Now that you've drained your mother dry and will
not sleep, I take you in my arms, brimful
six days old, little feared-for mouse.
Last week when you were still a fish
in the interior, I dreamed you thus:
The *douanier* brought you curled up in his cap
buttoned and suited like him, authority's prop
—a good Victorian child's myth—
and in his other hand a large round cheese
ready to the point of runniness.
At least there, says the dream, no mysteries.

Toward dawn I open my daughter's cupboard on
a choice of calming teas—*infusions*—
verbena, fennel, linden, camomile,
shift you on my shoulder and fill the kettle.
Age has conferred on me a certain grace.
You're a package I can rock and ease
from wakefulness to sleep. This skill comes back
like learning how to swim. Comes warm and quick
as first milk in the breasts. I comfort you.
Body to body my monkey-wit soaks through.

Later, I wind the outside shutters up.
You sleep mouse-mild, topped with camomile.
Daylight slips past the *douane*. I rinse my cup.
My daughter troubles sleep a little while
longer. The just-milked cows across the way
come down their hillside single file
and the dream, the lefthand gift of ripened brie
recurs, smelly, natural, and good
wanting only to be brought true
in your own time: your childhood.

Meridel LeSueur

I Light Your Streets

I am a crazy woman with a painted face
On the streets of Gallup.
I invite men into my grave
                    for a little wine.
I am a painted grave
Owl woman   hooting for callers in the night.
Black bats over the sun sing to me
The horned toad sleeps in my thighs,
My grandmothers gave me songs to heal
But the white man buys me cheap without song
        or word.
My dead children appear and I play with them.
Ridge of time in my grief—remembering
Who will claim the ruins?
                and the graves?
                    the corn maiden violated
As the land?
I am a child in my eroded dust.
I remember feathers of the hummingbird
And the virgin corn laughing on the cob.
Maize defend me
Prairie wheel around me
I run beneath the guns
            and the greedy eye
And hurricanes of white face knife me.
But like fox and smoke I gleam among the thrushes
And light your streets.

Shelter Him in Milk and Meadow

Out of the bitter herb   the splintered bone
You came child.
The nucleus arrived at gentle in him.
Cradle amidst satellites.
Orbit the tiny breast   the true ellipse of milk

133

Out of feudal darkness
          leaping into daffodils.
Into landscape out of ruin
Into pastures we never knew.
Hills of bluebells always ringing in
               the great wishes
   always arriving.
From mother clay the expansions of millions.
Brain and belly alight in spring solstice.
The common day turned marvelous.
And the hemisphere lighted by millions
               of children.
They will break the stone of bondage,
          of silence.
Summer squash and bean rejoice,
Pitch and cry of earth turns.
Approach of swarm, singing over horizons
          and peripheries.
Spreading body of one man or woman
          girdling the earth.
Sheltered bursting seed   make it safe
          for us forever.
The child perpetually appearing
          with us forever.
Shelter him in milk and meadow.
          Shelter.

Rites of Ancient Ripening

I am luminous with age
In my lap I hold the valley.
I see on the horizon what has been taken
What is gone   lies prone   fleshless.
In my breast I hold the middle valley
the corn kernels cry to me in the fields
               Take us home.
Like corn I cry in the last sunset
Gleam like plums.
               My bones shine in fever
Smoked with the fires of age.
Herbal, I contain the final juice,
Shadow, I crouch in the ash
               never breaking to fire.
Winter iron bough
               unseen my buds,
Hanging close I live in the beloved bone
Speaking in the marrow
               alive in green memory.

134

The light was brighter then.
Now spiders creep at my eyes' edge.
I peek between my fingers
                              at my father's dust.
The old stones have been taken away
                         there is no path.
The fathering fields are gone.
The wind is stronger than it used to be.
My stone feet far below me grip the dust.
I run and crouch in corners with thin dogs.
I tie myself to the children like a kite.
I fall and burst beneath the sacred human tree.
Release my seed and let me fall.
Toward the shadow of the great earth
                              let me fall.
Without child or man
                         I turn   I fall.
Into shadows,
                    the dancers are gone.
My salted pelt stirs at the final warmth
Pound me death
                         stretch and tan me death
Hang me up, ancestral shield
                         against the dark.
Burn and bright and take me quick.
Pod and light me into dark.

Are those flies or bats or mother eagles?
I shrink   I cringe
Trees tilt upon me like young men.
The bowl I made I cannot lift.
All is running past me.
The earth tilts and turns over me.
I am shrinking
     and lean against the warm walls of old summers.
With knees and chin I grip the dark
Swim out the shores of night in old meadows.
Remember   buffalo hunts
Great hunters returning
Councils of the fathers to be fed
Round sacred fires.
The faces of profound deer who
                         gave themselves for food.
We faced the east the golden pollened
                         sacrifice of brothers.
The little seeds of my children
                    with faces of mothers and fathers
Fold in my flesh
                    in future summers.
My body a canoe turning to stone
Moves among the bursting flowers of memory
Through the meadows of flowers and food,
I float and wave to my grandchildren in the

Tepis of many fires
        In the winter of the many slain
I hear the moaning.
I ground my corn daily
In my pestle many children
Summer grasses in my daughters
Strength and fathers in my sons
All was ground in the bodies bowl
     corn died to bread
      woman to child
        deer to the hunters.
Sires of our people
Wombs of mothering night
Guardian mothers of the corn
Hill borne torrents of the plains
Sing all grinding songs
  of healing herbs
Many tasselled summers
      Flower in my old bones
        Now.
Ceremonials of water and fire
Lodge me in the deep earth
  grind my harvested seed.
The rites of ancient ripening
Make my flesh plume
And summer winds stir in my smoked bowl.
Do not look for me still I return
      rot of greater summers
Struck from fire and dark,
Mother struck to future child.

Unbud me now
Unfurl me now
Flesh and fire
    burn
      requicken
        Death.

Denise Levertov

Making Peace

A voice from the dark called out,
        "The poets must give us
imagination of peace, to oust the intense, familiar
imagination of disaster.   Peace is not merely
the absence of war."
                        But peace, like a poem,
is not there ahead of itself,
can't be imagined before it is made,
can't be known except
in the words of its making.
grammar of justice,
syntax of mutual aid.
                        A feeling towards it,
dimly sensing a rhythm, is all we have
until we begin to utter its metaphors.
                        A line of peace might appear
if we restructure the sentence our lives are speaking:
shift from affirming profit and power,
question our needs, allow long pauses.
A cadence of peace might balance its weight
on a different fulcrum.
                        Peace, a presence,
an energy field more intense than war,
might pulse then
stanza by stanza into the world,
each act
a word, each word
a vibration of light, facets
of the forming crystal.

The Mockingbird of Mockingbirds

A greyish bird
the size perhaps of two plump sparrows,
fallen in some field,
soon flattened, a dry

mess of feathers—
and no one knows
this was a prince among his kind,
virtuoso of virtuosos,
lord of a thousand songs,
debonair, elaborate in invention, fantasist,
rival of nightingales.

The Absentee

Uninterpreted, the days
are falling.

The spring wind
is shaking and shaking the trees.

A nest of eggs,
a nest of deaths.

Falling
abandoned.

The palms rattle, the eucalypts
shed bark and blossom. Uninterpreted.

Zeroing In

"I am a landscape," he said,
"a landscape and a person walking in that landscape.
There are daunting cliffs there,
and plains glad in their way
of brown monotony. But especially
there are sinkholes, places
of sudden terror, of small circumference
and malevolent depths."
"I know," she said. "When I set forth
to walk in myself, as it might be
on a fine afternoon, forgetting,
sooner or later I come to where sedge
and clumps of white flowers, rue perhaps,
mark the bogland, and I know
there are quagmires there that can pull you
down, and sink you in bubbling mud."
"We had an old dog," he told her, "when I was a boy,

a good dog, friendly. But there was an injured spot
on his head, if you happened
just to touch it he'd jump up yelping
and bite you. He bit a young child,
they had to take him down to the vet's and destroy him."
"No one knows where it is," she said,
"and even by accident no one touches it.
It's inside my landscape, and only I, making my way
preoccupied through my life, crossing my hills,
sleeping on green moss of my own woods,
I myself without warning touch it,
and leap up at myself—"
"—or flinch back
just in time."
                    "Yes, we learn that.
It's not terror, it's pain we're talking about:
those places in us, like your dog's bruised head,
that are bruised forever, that time
never assuages, never."

Lyn Lifshin

Afterward

First we burned even
the birch covered with
punky mushrooms   the
dried pearwood   cherry
then wrapped in electric
blankets when houses
still had light. Later
we dressed in four
layers of wool. Suddenly
see thru nylon silk, those
sheer blouses young girls
saved for, were useless
as transparent   bikini
tops to a woman with
both breasts freshly
gone. It was strange
to be glad for drawers
of my dead husband's
sweaters, the youngest
wore them as a dress
when she could still walk

★   ★   ★

Television sets can't,
like dresser drawers,
be used for the smallest
coffins. With the trees
turning into hulks of
driftwood, squirrels
gnaw thru pebbles in
the roof. Grass stays
grey into what should
be summer. Those left
shiver in houses where
there's nothing left
to burn. A woman washing
her baby notices blood
in the sink   that the
child's hair tangles
around her ankles and

wrists like sea weed
or rope as candles
sputter   fall in
to themselves too

     ★   ★   ★

Cars that used to sound
like the sea   even thru the
ring of maples are suddenly
still. For days people waited
for phones to work   for
something to come thru the
snow on tv on channels as
unlike what they'd seen
as faces of those survivors
at Nagasaki. It took days
to see how what we couldn't
see was turning the grass
and leaves colorless as
petals pressed in a book.
Instead of cars, within
the month, we began to
hear digging. Women who
didn't know how roots
tangled under houses
had to dig graves   it
was like they were
scooping out parts of
themselves the way they'd
scooped out a squash and
stuffed it with croutons
and celery for Thanksgiving
to bury babies they'd held
weeks before, thankful
there was no direct hit
only to watch them roll
into a ball and turn
still as the branches.
Soon all the lawns
were mud

The No More Apologizing the No More Little Laughing Blues

apologizing for going to
school instead of having

a job that made money
or babies

pretending I took the bus
to an office   paper
clips in my ear
and never that I was
reading Wyatt
writing my own dreams
in the dust under the

apologizing for my
hair   wild gypsy
hair that fell out of
every clip   the way the
life I started dreaming
of did   apologizing for
the cats

you know if someone said my skirt
was too short well I explained
or said sorry   but never that
I finally loved my legs

I spent years apologizing for not
having babies   laughing
when someone pulled
a Baby Gerber jar out
of the closet and held it in
front of my eyes like it was
some damn cross or a star

I should have thrown that
thru the glass   I didn't
need to explain the music that
I liked   one friend said that's
noise   another said isn't denim for

children   well I laughed the apologizing
Oh I don't want no trouble laugh
over the years pretending to cook
pretending to like babying
my husband

the only place I said what I meant
was in poems   that green was like some
huge forbidden flower until it grew so
big it couldn't even fit in the house
pulled me out a window
with it toward Colorad

I apologized for being what
they thought a woman was by being
flattered when someone said
you write like a man and
for not being what they thought
a woman   for the cats and leaves

instead of booties   for the poems

when someone said well how much
do you get paid you know I pretended
pretended pretended   I
couldn't stop trying to please

the A the star that old good girl
on the forehead   the spanking
clean? well it haunted half my life
Luckily the poems had their own life

and mine finally followed
where the poems were growing
warm paper skin growing
finally in my real bed
until the room stopped spinning for
good the way it used to when I dressed
up in suits and hairspray

pretending to be all those things I
wasn't: teacher   good girl   lady
and wife   I was writing about cocks and
hair for years before I'd felt
when I was still making love just on
the sheets of paper

When the poems first came
out one woman I drove to school with
said I can't take this   another said
I don't know   this can't be the you
I know   the poems are so brutal   violent
which is the real

the man I was with moved to
the other side of the bed
this was worse than not having
babies   his mother said they
always knew I was a little odd

my books the way I wore my hair
the notebooks I carried to bed,
they said I never seemed like
one of them

my own family thought it was
ok but why couldn't I write of things
that were pleasant   they wanted to know
how much I got paid and why I didn't
write for The Atlantic

Look, I still have trouble saying
no   I want most of you to
like what I'm thinking,
to want my hair

It's true, I put a no smoking sign up
on the door but twice I have

gotten out ashtrays

But I have stopped being grateful to
be asked to read   or to have a hard
cock inside me
                        It's still not easy to get off the
phone   tell a young stoned poet
it's a bore to lie with the
phone in my ear like a
cold rock while he goes on
about the evils of money,
charging it to my phone

But now when I hear myself laugh
that apologizing laugh I know what
swallowing those black seeds can
do   and I spit them right out, just like tobacco
(now that's something men could always
do)   nothing good grows from saying
I'm sorry, sorry   only those dark
branches and they'll stab you from the inside

My Mother and the Bed

No, not that way she'd
say when I was 7, pulling
the bottom sheet smooth,
you've got to   saying
hospital corners

I wet the bed much later
than I should, until
just writing this I
hadn't thought of
the connection

My mother would never
sleep on sheets someone
else had   I never
saw any stains on hers
tho her bedroom was

a maze of powder   hair
pins   black dresses
Sometimes she brings her
own sheets to my house,
carries toilet seat covers

Did anybody sleep
in my   she always asks
Her sheets   her hair

smell of smoke but
she says the rooms here
smell funny

We drive at 3 am
slowly into Boston and
strip what looks like
two clean beds as the
sky gets light   I

smooth on the form
fitted flower bottom,
she redoes it

She thinks of my life
as a bed only she
can make right

Plymouth Women

Mist in the valley
the children sleep,
goat's milk on their
faces. A woman sprinkling
rose leaves in the linen
remembers being packed
in the boat   her mouth
bleeding. Learning to wait
like frogs in iced mud,
moving toward summer
that quietly. She thinks
of alewives, all silver,
their greyish green blending
with what's around them   not
knowing a stick from an
eel unless attacked.
Schooling and eating
moving in a wave,
having babies.
She thinks how the
solitary alewife is
lost and shuts her eyes

      *   *   *

Cat tails and rain
in one room, a cloud of
smoke and roses, dung

corn husks   the babies

crawling thru that green
the old bones

chickens squawk   she
puts her head down
on her knees

sees blood

the children with
loin cloths   fleas
yelping thru
maples

no barley   just this
damn corn   no
beer   I am
English   I want an
English bed   she

throws something
into the dust

feathers blow up
burn her lips

Thirty Miles West of Chicago

paint chips slowly
it's so still you
can almost hear it
pull from a porch

owls and cats
a man walks out
into fields   cold
grass claws like

fingers in a
wolf moon   corn
bristle   he
stands listening

watches   as if some
thing could grow
from putting a dead
child in the ground

Audre Lorde

Sisters in Arms

The edge of our bed was a wide grid
where your 15 year old daughter was hanging
gut-sprung on police wheels
a cablegram nailed to the wood
next to a map of the Western Reserve
I could not return with you to bury the body
reconstruct your nightly cardboards
against the seeping Transvaal cold
I could not plant the other limpet mine
against a wall at the railroad station
nor carry either of your souls back from the river
in a calabash upon my head
so I bought you a ticket to Durban
on my American Express
and we lay together
in the first light of a new season.

Now clearing roughage from my autumn garden
cow-sorrel   over-grown rocket gone to seed
I reach for a taste of today
the New York Times finally mentions your country
a half-page story
of the first white south african killed in the "unrest"
Not of Black children massacred at Sebonkeng
six-year-olds imprisoned for threatening the state
not of Thabo Sibeko, first-grader, in his own blood
on his grandmother's parlour floor
Joyce, nine, trying to crawl to him
shitting through her navel
not of a three week old infant, nameless
lost under the burned beds of Tembisa
my hand comes down like a brown vise over the marigolds
reckless through despair
we were two Black women touching our flame
and we left our dead behind us
I hovered   you rose   the last ritual of healing
"It is spring," you whispered
"I sold the ticket for guns and sulfur
 I leave for home tomorrow"
and where ever I touch you
I lick cold from my fingers

taste rage
like salt from the lips of a woman
who has killed too often to forget
and carries each death in her eyes
your mouth a parting orchid
"Someday you will come to *my* country
and we will fight side by side?"

Keys jingle in my passageway   threatening
whatever is coming belongs here
I reach for your sweetness
but silence explodes like a pregnant belly
into my face
a vomit of nevers.

Mmanthatisi* turns away from the cloth
her daughters-in-law are dyeing
the baby drools milk from her breast
she hands him half-asleep to his sister
dresses again for war
knowing the men will follow.
In the intricate Maseru** twilights
quick   sad   vital
she maps the next day's battle
dreams of Durban***   sometimes
visions the deep wry song of beach pebbles
running after the sea

*M-*man-tha-tisi:* warrior queen and leader of the Tlokwa (Sotho) people
during the *mfecane* (crushing), one of the greatest crises in southern
African history. Sotho now lives in the Orange Free State, SA.
**Ma-*se-ru:* scene of a great Tlokwa battle and now the capital of
Lesotho.
***Durban:* Indian Ocean seaport and resort area in Natal Province, SA.

This Urn Contains Earth from German Concentration Camps

Plotensee Memorial, West Berlin, 1984

Dark grey
the stone wall hangs
self-conscious wreaths
the heavy breath of gaudy Berlin roses
"The Vice Chancellor Remembers
The Heroic Generals Of The Resistance"
and before a well-trimmed hedge
unpolished granite
tall as my daughter and twice around

Neatness
wiping memories   payment
from the air.

Midsummer's Eve beside a lake
keen   the smell of quiet
children straggling homeward
the rough precisions of earth
beneath my rump
in a hollow root of the dead elm
a brown rabbit kindles.

The picnic is over
reluctantly
I stand   pick up my blanket
and flip into the bowl of still-warm corn
a writhing waterbug
cracked open   pale eggs oozing
quiet
from the smash

Earth
not the unremarkable ash
of fussy thin-boned infants
and adolescent Jewish girls
liming the Ravensbruck potatoes
careful and monsterless
this urn makes nothing
easy
to say.

Hanging Fire

I am fourteen
and my skin has betrayed me
the boy I cannot live without
still sucks his thumb
in secret
how comes my knees are
always so ashy
what if I die
before morning
and momma's in the bedroom
with the door closed.

I have to learn how to dance
in time for the next party
my room is too small for me
suppose I die before graduation
they will sing sad melodies

but finally
tell the truth about me
There is nothing I want to do
and too much
that has to be done
and momma's in the bedroom
with the door closed.

Nobody even stops to think
about my side of it
I should have been on Math Team
my marks were better than his
why do I have to be
the one
wearing braces
I have nothing to wear tomorrow
will I live long enough
to grow up
and momma's in the bedroom
with the door closed.

Chain

News item: Two girls, fifteen and sixteen, were sent to foster homes,
because they had borne children by their natural father. Later, they
petitioned the New York courts to be returned to their parents, who,
the girls said, loved them. And the courts did so.

Faces surround me that have no smell or color no time
only strange laughing testaments
vomiting promise like love
but look at the skeleton children
advancing against us
beneath their faces there is no sunlight
no darkness
no heart remains
no legends
to bring them back as women
into their bodies at dawn.

Look at the skeleton children
advancing against us
we will find womanhood
in their eyes
as they cry
which of you bore me
will love me
will claim my blindness as yours
and which of you marches to battle
from between my legs?

II

On the porch outside my door
girls are lying
like felled maples in the path of my feet
I cannot step past them nor over them
their slim bodies roll like smooth tree trunks
repeating themselves over and over
until my porch is covered with the bodies
of young girls.
Some have a child in their arms.
To what death shall I look for comfort?
Which mirror to break or mourn?

Two girls repeat themselves in my doorway
their eyes are not stone.
Their flesh is not wood nor steel
but I can not touch them.
Shall I warn them of night
or offer them bread
or a song?
They are sisters. Their father has known
them over and over. The twins they carry
are his. Whose death shall we mourn
in the forest
unburied?
Winter has come and the children are dying.

One begs me to hold her between my breasts
Oh write me a poem mother
here, over my flesh
get your words upon me
as he got this child upon me
our father lover
thief in the night
do not be so angry with us. We told him
your bed was wider
but he said if we did it then
we would be his
good children if we did it
then he would love us
oh make us a poem mother
that will tell us his name
in your language
is he father or lover
we will leave your word
for our children
engraved on a whip or a golden scissors
to tell them the lies
of their birth.

Another says mother
I am holding your place.
Do you know me better than I knew him
or myself?

Am I his daughter or girlfriend
am I your child or your rival
you wish to be gone from his bed?
Here is your granddaughter mother
give us your blessing before I sleep
what other secrets
do you have to tell me
how do I learn to love her
as you have loved me?

The Women of Dan Dance with Swords in their Hands to Mark the Time When They Were Warriors

I did not fall from the sky
I
nor descend like a plague of locusts
to drink color and strength from the earth
and I do not come like rain
as a tribute or symbol for earth's becoming
I come as a woman
dark and open
some times I fall like night
softly
and terrible
only when I must die
in order to rise again.

I do not come like a secret warrior
with an unsheathed sword in my mouth
hidden behind my tongue
slicing my throat to ribbons
of service with a smile
while the blood runs
down and out
through holes in the two sacred mounds
on my chest.

I come like a woman
who I am
spreading out through nights
laughter and promise
and dark heat
warming whatever I touch
that is living
consuming
only
what is already dead.

Cynthia Macdonald

By the Sea

This is the day of the night it began to turn,
Like milk, slightly sour, still
So close to freshness one is not sure if
The tongue or the cream is at fault.

He, floundering back toward the bay
Like a suddenly beached fish, cannot see that
The water has changed, as if the dairy plant
Behind him had confused its flows, releasing
All its curds the way defective plants can.

He, lunging toward water, does not know,
Has never had to, that even with the ocean's
Grand dilution the balance of fluids has been
Slightly altered, like the shift of residue in
The ear's circular canals. I, experienced
In acute pain, too full of acuity, know
But do not know why milk
Spoils when it seems fresh.

"Your family has had bad luck," he said last night
Just before he found the clocks had stopped
And indicted the house again. Perhaps that is it.
The stroke of his hand makes time seamless but
The clock strikes, even if unheard, and blood poisoning
(Which killed my father's mother when she used
A knitting needle on the fetus, which killed
My uncle when, even with an open cut, he wore
Blue socks) moves through me into him as we come together.

Louis Pasteur, I beg you, seal us in a bottle,
Let us remain bacilli free, save us from relative
Poisons and deaths, from what may prey on us.

It takes awhile to read the ocean,
To see that the prayer is the agent of
What is prayed against. But we've caught it
Early. Let's stop stamping, like spoiled children,
Trying to seal the bargain. Instead
Let's clap our flippers (how I admire
The silvery gloss of sun on your body), spin
Bottles on our noses, beg for
Kippers, and kiss by the beautiful sea.

Objets D'Art

When I was seventeen, a man in the Dakar Station
Men's Room (I couldn't read the signs) said to me:
You're a real ball cutter. I thought about that
For months and finally decided
He was right. Once I knew that was my thing,
Or whatever we would have said in those days,
I began to perfect my methods. Until then
I had never thought of trophies. Preservation
Was at first a problem: pickling worked
But was a lot of trouble. Freezing
Proved to be the answer. I had to buy
A second freezer just last year; the first
Was filled with rows and rows of
Pink and purple lumps encased in Saran wrap.

I have more subjects than I can handle,
But only volunteers. It is an art like hypnosis
Which cannot be imposed on the unwilling victim.
If you desire further information about the process and
The benefits, please drop in any night from nine to twelve.
My place is east of Third on Fifty-sixth.
You'll know it by the three gold ones over the door.

Instruction from Bly

The poet told me if I was serious
I must isolate myself for at least a year—
Not become a hermit, but leave
My family, job, friends—so I did. My sister
Agreed to take over as mother though not
As wife. I wonder if she will become that too;
I've always thought maybe she didn't marry
Because she wanted Howard herself. So I
Have moved here to North Dakota where
I work in a gas station, the only woman s.s.
Attendant in ND. Nowhere could be more isolated
And no job could: whistles and "baby
Pump some of that to me" crack in the cold
Or melt in the summer.

       try   try   try
    crycry   crycry   crycry   cry

I have been here seven months. Poetry should
Be flowing from my navel by now, if . . .
Out of the solitude, I expected I would erect
Something magnificent, the feminine analogue

Of Jeffer's tower. Maybe it would have gone
Into the ground instead of up.

      s   k   y
            high

I have discovered I drink when I am solitary. I
Have discovered I can read page ninety-two of
Remembrance of Things Past twenty times in solitary
Without ever reading it. If I don't die of alcoholism.
I will of cholesterol: solitary cooking.

      fryfryfry   fryfry   fryfryfryfry   frydie

Rhyme is important, my way of keeping
A grip on things. I wonder if the poet meant
It would all happen after I left, or if he is a sadist
Who wants to send all those stupid enough to sit
At his feet to N.D. or S.D. or West Va.,
Hazing before possible joining. I wonder if Jean
Is in the double bed.

                  tower
                  power

I cannot think about the children, but I
Do all the time. "Women artists fail
Because they have babies." The last thing I wrote
Was "The Children at the Beach" and that was over
A month ago. I am alone so I have to have company so
I turn on TV; at home
I only turned it off.

                thumbtacks   processionals
                        north
                        red

It is time to go to work. First I need a drink. I consider
The Smirnoff bottle on the coffee table; a fly
Lands on it. And then it all happens: the life
Of that bottle flashes before me. Little by little.
Or quickly, it is used up; empty, as clear as it was
Full, it journeys to the dump; it rests upon the mounds of
Beautiful excess where what we are—
Sunflowers, grass, sand—
Is joined to what we make—
Cans, tires and it itself in every form of bottle.
I put on my s.s. coveralls, a saffron robe, knowing I have found
What I was sent to find. The sky speaks to me; the sound
Of the cars on Highway 2 is a song. Soon I will see the pumps,
Those curved rectangles shaped like the U.S. and smell the gas,
Our incense. O country, O moon, O stars,
O american rhyme is yours is mine is ours.

Colleen J. McElroy

Tapestries

when I was eight I listened to stories of love
and etiquette while my mother's sisters
sat on grandma's horsehair sofa
naked under their starched dresses
words flew from their fingers
in a dance as old as the moon
but I dreamed of other places
of dark bodies bending
to a language too dreamlike
and concise to decode

above them a tapestry desert stretched
into distant corners where I imagined
ancient rituals grotesque and graceful
conjuring up the moon flecked
seasons of the earth
but my mother's sisters wove tales
that collapsed the world
into sarcastic snips of language
their black thighs opened
billows of powdery musk
rising from their legs like dust
from some raw and haunting land

I had a choice
two scenes   their dark secrets
spread for my viewing
the usual desert   palm trees camels
a cautious rug merchant   one hand
on the tent, face turned toward the horizon
turning back like Thomas Jefferson
towards his black *anima*, like Lot's wife
or the thousands of black women
who fled slavery preferring instead
the monastic beds of the River Niger

it is said those waters flowed
red for years
shades of ochre fuchsia and russet
as layers of blood sifted
through the silt of the river
the velvet sands on that tapestry
were red and flowed into all corners

my aunts sat in a line beneath this scene
refusing to turn back
wagging their heads against the world's sins

I have seen more than my aunts dared to see
how each Sunday they sat bare assed and defiant
their dark female caverns linking thighs
into matching hills of lemon ebony and mocha flesh
how the wooden humps reflected off my grandmother's
whalebone hairpins when she leaned into the light
the crumbling walls of the city of Benin
Kamehameha's feathered cape in the Bishop museum

I have seen Buenos Aires
where ladies dine inside their mirrors
Berlin where my blackness
was examined in six languages
Bogotá where there are no traffic signals
and even pregnant women are targets
fat clumsy figures playing toreador
with foreign made limousines

in the Middle East fairy chimneys
of volcanic tuffs spiral into the sunlight
their colors glowing like stained glass
in the half light of the desert
shades of ochre russet and ebony
thrust into tidal waves of magma
and firestorm of ash
like beads on a rosary linking
village to village

when I was eight my prudish aunts
sat like squat pigeons on the horsehair sofa
brazen under their stiff collared dresses
and I gathered dreams of love
from a tapestry woven in velvet
a blood colored crescent moon, three palm trees
two burgundy camels, all arched around
a shadowy figure entering a tent
the world behind him barren and flat

some days pressed by the low ceiling
of a troubled sky I drift back to that room
the scene spreads before me
the delicate red tracery
of some ancient artisan
clinging to thread bare spots
the nomad who is forever coming home
the tent with its doorway of secrets
the dark face turned toward the corner
staring at some fixed point
on the amber horizon of that velvet desert
as if to say how vast
and naked the world seems to be

157

It Ain't Blues That Blows an Ill Wind

(Valaida Snow: Circa 1930)

> my wish . . . o to be a dragon
> a symbol of power of heaven
> of silkworm size. . . .
> > Marianne Moore

Your bold voice and the light suspended above a trumpet,
Golden as the world-full season of new-blue jazz
That sported you to Europe's sport of kings and dandies.
You caught the last of that royal light and folks
Who boop-de-dooed as if the endless sky were home,
And you a name like wind, a bird flown out of hand.

Valaida, five-note sheets of sound shaped by your hand.
You a blackbird righteously swinging low on a mean trumpet,
And in your voice the loose glue of pre-war years with home
Any crazy route from here to China that followed jazz.
Honey, your sweet lips razz-ma-tazzed all kinds of folks,
Brown sugar that made them believe the world was dandy.

Backstage you ached along with all those other dancing dandies
Who needed one more footlight and rooms of noisy bands
To make them forget hard times leeching land and home folks.
Oh chile, the time was ripe for Queen Wilhelmina's trumpet,
Long notes held longer than any man as you jazzed
Up the stage, seven pairs of shoes to carry you home.

Girls, they loved your dance of the seven shoes back home,
Your soft shoe, tap, adagio, high-hat rhythms swell and dandy,
But war owns no stage for the good life and all that jazz.
This time the Man goose-stepped with swastika and iron hand
Booking you in a death camp without Wilhelmina's golden
> trumpet,
And no one there to say European wars ever took black folks.

Blackbirds 1934 and Chocolate Dandies still remembered by
> folks,
While the world was going to hell in a basket and homes
Burned hotter than any blues you wailed on that golden trumpet.
A war chasing sane men from crowds of gin roaring dandies
With leaflets claiming the world as the new Germany in each
> hand,
15 lashes a day and a mandate ending your beloved age of jazz.

Your scat-beat and spiffy voice almost died when jazz
Was lost in a world turned deaf to blacks, jews and non-white
> folks,
Upside down this life you nearly forgot the feel of trumpet in hand,
3 years camp left 74 pounds before the SS Gripsholm took you
> home
But the last thing they take is memory, the silky feel of trumpet.
Girl, you owned the music, the uncommon furs, cars and royal
> dandies.

Valaida, Queen of the Trumpet, of hot snow, hotcha, and hot
jazz.
Little Louis of the dandies, your sassy voice made you one of the
folks,
Welcomed home from a sky unmistakably dark, blacker ever than
your hands.

Why We Sometimes Paint by Numbers

for Pesha and Leslie

in 1958 in Kansas
wanting so much to be an artist
I painted the summer by numbers
from June to August
planted an indoor garden
threw the babies out of their room
laid a bedrock of crushed bricks
flushed gravel into the soil fill
then laced the next layer with charcoal
six weeks of callouses heaved top
soil in by the shovelsful
my onions were beginning to bud
when the house inspectors arrived

sometimes it is expensive to become
what we are
alive in that 2.4 house
with one husband and two babies
where women who so desperately
wanted love learned to hate
what I wished for was so private
I never saw myself standing
on the sheer edge of poems
or listening to the rhapsodic
slow circles of guitars
played to the echoes of mad Kansas
summers all trapped in livid colors
on a mad artist's canvas

the women we have known
are singing in the shadows
they are eating bits of light
savoring it on their tongues
like scallions or cloves
in the blue-grey of dusk
they swallow the dark
and grow thick as velvet
some come to this late in life
they learn never to trust

smiling children
they grow strong and do not fail
to mince sharp words
or share morsels of lost lovers

this is what you have learned
I have seen in your looks
that sweet secret women
give women when they know
all too well how things grow quickly
and madly and the electric
taste of flesh and loving ourselves
in the femaleness of it all
and how we fight the foetal
curl of old age
and how we have all ached
to throw dirt through a window
to build our own world
if for nothing but the onions

Defining It for Vanessa

She is too young to eat
chocolates
they blossom on her black face
like peppercorns
she is 16 and dreams
of the alphabet stitched
to the winter wool
of teenage gladiators
in single capital letters
she leans across the table
and asks us older ladies
about love and the future
but we cannot see past
a few days at any time
we are pregnant
with memories
and move slowly
like Egyptian geese grazing

we tell her put Xmas
in your eyes
and keep your voice low
knowing this answer
as insane as any
will soothe her
while she dreams
wrapped like a mummy

inside her flowered sheets
she thinks we hold secrets
and watches us closely
as we shop for dried flowers
lovely center pieces
for the best china
we tell her smiling

later when we describe
our little aches and pains
she turns away
puzzled by antidotes
of blues reds and greens
we tell her how the reds
stick like anger
or clock the tides of the moon
we tell her how she'll guard
her lovely eyes
how only in her blackness
will she grow
large as the moon
we tell how women
with whiskey voices
will try to stop her
how men will strip her clean
of secrets
how the flesh hurts
how the world does not end
with the body
but the longing for it

Mary Mackey

Desire

in my dreams
I hold my lovers
next to me all at once
and ask them

what was it I desired?

my hands are full
of their heads
like bunches of cut roses
blond hair, brown hair, red, black,
their eyes are pools of bewilderment
staring up at me
from the bouquet

what was it I desired?
I ask again

was it your bodies?
did I hope by draping
your flesh over me
I could escape
boredom
loneliness
gray hairs shooting
towards me
from the future
like thin arrows?
did I think I could escape,
by taking your breath
into my mouth,
did I think I could escape
the responsibility
of breathing?

what did I desire in you?

sex
knowledge?
power?
love?

did I expect the clouds to
crack

and blue moths to fly out of the stars?
did I expect a voice
to call to me
saying
"Here at last is the answer."

what
I yell at them
shaking my lovers
what did I desire in you?

their ears fall off like petals
they shed their faces
in a pile at my feet
their bewildered eyes
pucker and close
centers of fallen flowers

the last face
floats down
circling in the darkness
at my feet

what did I desire in you? I whisper

the stems of their bodies
dry in my hands.

from Arabesque:
Five poems for women without children

First Position

don't make so much
noise dear
the nurses say to the woman
three days in labor
white scum on her lips

outside the streets are hot
and flat and infinite
and time is only marked
by the dilation of pain

you're acting like a little girl
the doctor tells her
you don't hurt
hips like a cow
you were born to bear

his own stomach
is pegged across his thighs
like a well-tanned skin
he catches the little bloody
head in his hands

love this
he tells her
even the bones
were made from your teeth

Second Position

mix honey and semen
in a golden cup

place blood in a cross
on your lips

take off your skirt
and run naked
through the new corn

eat liver and brown bread
let your womb be opened
with a knife

greet your husband with a smile
wear a new negligée

take your temperature
every day

put crushed chili peppers
between your legs

copulate with a snake
confess your sins

cover your body with pitch

drink water from a hollow stump

eat the clay from a newly dug grave

there are children under your skin
you are holding them back
we have come to collect
a tax on your life
you owe us sons

you say you are trying
but we do not believe you
we are waiting here under your bed

for a birth
and a body
and the smell of fresh blood.

Grande Jetée

some rhythms must remain unbroken

like a dancer in an
arabesque
some women cannot carry
a child
in their arms

some come to salvation
drawn by the hands of small children

some can only make their leaps

alone.

Elizabeth McKim

i have always been

                          i have always been
          a lonely woman
even in the beginning
        not understanding the language
        of men
            always wanting them to see me

          always hiding from them
  hoping they will not crush me with their anger
      trying to make them smile
          with my masks
          and my veils
            my dancing costumes
              my magic and my bells
so they would stop scaring me
      so they would fall asleep
          so I could take their power

To Stay Alive

A man and a woman
appear
each night
wearing no clothes
carrying small satchels
full of poems
outside
the wind hurts
it is january
and strong
they go to the sea
and taste salt
they go to the market
and trade the salt
for smelts
they go to the bed

and trade the fish
for love
only the most resourceful
have any chance
at all

Creaming

careening
I'm roaming
over leaves and cafeterias
I'm doing a breathing boogie
through the roar of old cities
At last my friend
you see me as I am
in this half-lit room
greened and galloping

paisley skirts hiked up above my waist
sitting in this old sling-back chair
neither desperate nor dizzy
talking to you old friend
who at last will see me as I am
Don't doubt the flush of my poem
the backbone of my dreaming
This is not all puff and pulp
This is art
This is my spine
Take a look
I'm winging it now
and you can come along
Behind this mask there is none
Doors open and ache
The clam goes on strike
Morning glories give up religion
Other women join me
Turns out we are all
Revolutionary Exhibitionists!
Do you know we take baths together
slip those sponges
over all our skins
and sing for hours
It is Monday Monday
and we are not afraid!

Donna Masini

Rubber

The sun made diamonds on the white sidewalk
at Holy Cross Cemetery
we were sweating so hard
there was a red stain on my mother
but she still
looked like a lady.
She did not move.

At home she cried
prying her Playtex Longline rubber girdle
off white thighs
welded by the sun
it left her lined
like the butcher chart
that marks the parts of a cow
the choice cut
I wanted to rub her.
She smelled like burning dolls.

Hands

I watch your daughter two years old
crashing a glass hand onto the table
a strange thing for an ashtray
I cannot put my cigarette out in its palm
as she bangs the severed hand you say
only she could make you go back there
to Chile
where no strange man will take her
into his hands like a piece of bread
tear her apart   hold her to his mouth.

It is safe there you say
there might be a blackout   the lights go down
someone in evening dress fumbles for candles
everyone laughs   it has happened before

No one questions the gunshots in the distance.

We surround your table
compliment you on the colors of your meal
you are an artist   execute large
shapes on hand made paper
in each a black form emerges from a fleshy pink
like an inky shark hungry for blood
I see your   hands stained with beaten pulp
I ask about the stadium
what the papers have said
I say nothing of blood on the walls
hair in the trees
the piles of human parts stacked in the yards
nothing to make us see
your adhesive eyes hold your daughter
not wanting to know
you hand me a glass of pisco
you say it makes you dream

and your smile starts to remind me
of those indoor parking garages
the yellow line curving
into a deep tunnel of grey
white tile along the curved wall of the ramp
going down and further down until
I think you have swallowed me.

The paper says "the destiny of Chile
is in Chilean hands   good hands"
cut off from your country
I believe you do not know
as I do not know the churches burned in Alabama
the women dying in the bronx
the murders in the subways
we do not question
the gunshots in the distance.

Cherry Ice

Dipping our fingers in cups of cherry ice
we talked about "those places" peeling
our questions to afternoons
of sweet tarts, hershey's kisses and mimosa pods
when we still did not know what we were.
Summer days on Staten Island were
dirty words in the dictionary
bicycle rides to new developments
leaving our block where everything was familiar
and at night the citronella burned into our parents' conversations

and they forgot to call us in.
Dizzy with fireflies we were eager
to take our secret games into our hands
burrow ourselves inside their sticky palms.
Summer encouraged us
for two months the mimosa dropped
its feathered pinks onto the lawn
each tickle took us closer to the backyard where
we whispered, yes. I'm taking off my blouse.
Don't turn around. I'm almost naked.
Deep in the salty darkness peeking
at the rest of our lives.

Sharon Olds

Why My Mother Made Me

Maybe I am what she always wanted,
my father as a woman,
maybe I am what she wanted to be
when she first saw him, tall and smart,
standing there in the college yard with the
hard male light of 1937
shining on his black hair. She wanted that
power. She wanted that size. She pulled and
pulled through him as if he were dark
bourbon taffy, she pulled and pulled and
pulled through his body until she drew me out,
amber and gleaming, her life after her life.
Maybe I am the way I am
because she wanted exactly that,
wanted there to be a woman
a lot like her, but who would not hold back, so she
pressed herself hard against him,
pressed and pressed the clear soft
ball of herself like a stick of beaten cream
against his stained sour steel grater
until I came out on the other side of his body,
a big woman, stained, sour, sharp,
but with that milk at the center of my nature.
I lie here now as I once lay
in the crook of her arm, her creature,
and I feel her looking down into me the way the
maker of a sword gazes at his face in the
steel of the blade.

My Mother's College

I am going to be there where her body was when it was
perfect—young, sealed, soft,
no passage had been torn in it yet for my
hard head to enter this world, she was
sweet and whole as my daughter's body,

she walked on those lawns. Small and curled as a
fox she sat in a warm window-seat,
it makes me sick with desire to think of her,
my first love—when I lay stunned and
tiny in her arms I thought she was the whole world,
a world of heat, silky flesh and milk
and that huge heart-beat. But there she had no
children, no one was weaker than she,
she had all her beauty and none of her power, she
moved slowly under the arches
literally singing. Half of me was
deep in her body like an Easter egg
with my name on it, gold with red script—
maybe the happiest time of my life as I
glided above the gravel paths
deep in the center of the dark universe.
I want to thank the stones she touched,
I want to visit the chapel with its stained and
glassy God, the pews rubbed with the
stolen homes of bees, I want to
love her when she had not hurt anyone yet,
she had never lifted a finger to me—
all that had been done to her she
held, still, in her delicate fresh
strong body, where her will rose up like
fire and her fear banked it with sand as she
lay on her stomach, still a child, really,
studying for finals, and before the dance she
washed her hair and rinsed it with lemon and then
shook her head so the whole inside of her
tiny room was flecked with sour bright citrus.

I Cannot Forget the Woman in the Mirror

Backwards and upside down in the twilight, that
woman on all fours, her head
dangling and suffused, her lean
haunches, the area of darkness, the flanks and
ass narrow and pale as a deer's and those
breasts hanging down toward the center of the earth like
    plummets, when I
swayed from side to side they swayed, it was
so dark I couldn't tell if they were gold or
plum or rose. I cannot get over her
moving toward him upside down in the mirror like a
fly on the ceiling, her head hanging down and her
tongue long and dark as an anteater's

going toward his body, she was so clearly an
animal, she was an Iroquois scout creeping
naked and noiseless, and when I looked at her
she looked at me so directly, her eyes so
dark, her stare said to me
I belong here, this is mine, I am living out my
true life on this earth.

The Moment of My Father's Death

When he breathed his last breath it was he,
my father, although he was so transformed
no one who had not been with him
for the last hours would know him, the gold
skin luminous as cold animal fat,
the eyes cast all the way back into his head,
the whites gleaming like a white iris, the
nose that grew thinner and thinner every minute, the
open mouth racked open with that
tongue in it like all the heartbreak of the mortal,
a tongue so dried, scalloped, darkened and
material. You could see the mucus
risen like gorge into the back of his mouth
but it was he, the huge slack yellow arms,
the spots of blood under the skin
black and precise, we had come this far with him
step by step, it was he, his last
breath was his, not taken with desire but
his, light as the sphere of a dandelion seed
coming out of his mouth and floating across the room.
Then the nurse pulled up his gown and
listened for his heart, I saw his stomach
silvery and hairy, it was his stomach, she
moved to the foot of the bed and stood there, she
did not shake her head she stood and
nodded at me. And for a minute it was fully
he, my father, dead but completely
himself, a man with an open mouth and
no breath, gold skin and
black spots on his arms, I kissed him and
spoke to him. He looked like someone
killed in a violent bloodless struggle, all that
strain in his neck, that look of pulling back, that
stillness he seemed to be holding at first and
then it was holding him, the skin
tightened slightly around his whole body
as if the purely phsyical were claiming him,

and then it was not my father,
it was not a man, it was not an animal, I
stood and ran my hand through the silver hair,
plunged my fingers into it gently and
lifted them up slowly through the grey
waves of it, the unliving glistening
matter of this world.

Brenda Marie Osbey

The Bone Step-Women

i do not hear the words
the women speak on touro street
i only see them moving
in vertical lines
their hands angled out
from their hips and thighs

i know they are singing
but i do not know the song.

they separate my bones
into neat white stacks
moving them in the dust
like bits of stone
one finds something of interest
in the way they are cast
ramshackle
on the side of the road
stirs them into dustclouds
sends up a slipshod rain
her own aging joints
toil toward motion

she is dancing in the dust
between the alleys of my bones.

In These Houses of Swift Easy Women

In the room the women come and go talking of Michelangelo.
T.S. Eliot,
The Love Song of J. Alfred Prufrock

in these houses
of swift easy women
drapes and the thin panels between them
hug to the walls—
some promise of remembering,
litanies of minor

pleasures and comforts.

these women know subtlety
sleight of hand
cane liquor
island songs
the poetry of soundlessness.

a man could get lost
in such a house as this
could lose his way
his grasp of the world
between the front room
and the crepe myrtle trees out back.

The Wastrel-Woman Poem

she goes out in the night again
wastreling about
her thin-woman blues
slung over one shoulder
an empty satchel
one carries out of habit.

the first time you see her
you think her body
opens some new forbidden zone
you think she has something to do with you
she never does.
at least not the way you mean.
not here.
not any more.
lives ago perhaps
she would have been
your second cousin
a lover who murdered you
a woman who passed you on market-day
but never spoke
threw bones to the ground
or stepped over you
as though you were dust or air
some spirit she knew of
but did not counsel.

the first time you see her
a story begins
that has nothing to do with you:
a woman uncle feather knew
and never told you of
you were so young

and one day he lost the connection
between your question
and her name

her name could have been anything
but you never would know
she would pass
and look into your eyes
directly
as if you were not there
as if she knew it
and would not tell.

tak-o-me-la
tak-o-me-la

something you hear when she passes
sounds from another living
but there she is
wastreling about you

someone calls to you
you watch your thin-woman move
between baskets of fish
and date-wine bottles

you turn to answer

heart like a brick
down between your knees.

Alicia Ostriker

April One

> Who would have thought this shrivell'd heart
> Would have recover'd greenness?
> **George Herbert**

Can't believe it
A million New Jersey hearts whispering rain rain go away
For four days straight
So then it snowed
That was bizarre but that was yesterday
Today the divine old man and the divine old woman
Are holding up the tent of the sky
To let sunlight in and fresh fresh air
Can't believe it, it makes me even love Princeton
Even me love Princeton
where of course there are no crocuses in *my* yard yet today
But all up Prospect where I bike to the Library
In other people's yards there are excellent crocuses
In clumps and clusters like clusters of schoolgirls
Giggling and straightening their spines
When somebody passes so their pointy breasts will show
And isn't that good enough
Isn't it good the wetness is drying so fast today it's
As if robbers took it under their armpits and ran
Plus absolutely redbuds
Abruptly born and where the Library doesn't say
Welcome, oho, welcome
Alicia, my pigeon, I am your tidy sanctuary, your familiar
Teacherly cocoon, your protection— no, it's horrible, it smells
Like corpses, it smells like mildew
Bless it, it shoves me out
Into the plentiful breeze
So I can look some more, not at the George Segal
Abraham about to slay Isaac in poignant life size bronze
Commemorating the holy slaughter
Of the young by the withered fanatic old,
But instead where youthful people have popped out
In bunches and throw loops of invigorating glances
In all directions at each other, weaving
The intangible web of sex until
I feel capacious and insatiable as the sea
Seeking blue eyes like Paul Newman's
Brown eyes to drown in me

I am a cup
That runneth over full of empty happiness
Ready to be grateful
To all the men who ever made me happy
I hope I did them some permanent good
The women and children too
And my other children, my students,
The ones who are not stupid, who write poetry like whipped
                                                          cream
Like clouds when you look at clouds from an airplane window
After a double bourbon and a half
The ones who understand Conrad and Margaret Atwood
Keats and Emily Dickinson, after great pain
A formal feeling comes, so when you are happy
You want to take your clothes off
And defy grammar and punctuation, I can't
Believe it today I am not flipping through
My grievance cards, no poverty,
No torture, no arms buildup, no corporation, executive bathrooms
No bone to pick with my husband that might choke me in future,
No foolish President, I am feeding
Nobody my anger dog food
I am in my middle
Forties this is the middle of my poem
And I am remembering that my nation is not at war
And I have to bicycle some more. I bicycle down
Witherspoon Street to my mother's house
To return her poems
And tell her I loved them
Sincerely, can't believe it
Chit chat, chit chat about her flowers
her immortal future kohlrabi.
Then I have to go home and I haven't stopped
Smiling and on Leigh Street two young black men are under
A jacked-up Pontiac
My favorite springtime image, human and metal, since brass
Nor stone like the Library nor something nor boundless sea
But sad mortality oersways its power, oh yeah
How with this rage shall beauty hold a plea (cop a plea?
Must be a legal metaphor in here)
How with this rage shall beauty hold a plea
Whose action is no stronger than a flower,
Oh, Willie baby, I'd like to tell you how
Today without effort
I am this blue veined crocus
Straightening up on her spine,
Today without effort I uphold my half of the sky
Because here is the way it is all over New Jersey:
In the tops of the redbud trees
Small boys are playing ball
In the pink light
And under the ground
Even the dead people are combing their hair.

Everywoman Her Own Theology

I am nailing them up to the cathedral door
Like Martin Luther. Actually, no,
I don't want to resemble that *Schmutzkopf*
(See Erik Erikson and N.O. Brown
On the Reformer's anal aberrations,
Not to mention his hatred of Jews and peasants),
So I am thumbtacking these ninety-five
Theses to the bulletin board in my kitchen.

My proposals, or should I say requirements,
Include at least one image of a god,
Virile, beard optional, one of a goddess,
Nubile, breast size approximating mine,
One divine baby, one lion, one lamb,
All nude as figs, all dancing wildly,
All shining. Reproducible
In marble, metal, in fact any material.

Ethically, I am looking for
An absolute endorsement of loving-kindness.
No loopholes except maybe mosquitoes.
Virtue and sin will henceforth be discouraged,
Along with suffering and martyrdom.
There will be no concept of infidels;
Consequently the faithful must entertain
Themselves some other way than killing infidels.

And so forth and so on. I understand
This piece of paper is going to be
Spattered with wine one night at a party
And covered over with newer pieces of paper.
That is how it goes with bulletin boards.
Nevertheless it will be there.
Like an invitation, like a chalk pentangle,
It will emanate certain occult vibrations.

If something sacred wants to swoop from the universe
Through a ceiling, and materialize,
Folding its silver wings,
In a kitchen, and bump its chest against mine,
My paper will tell this being where to find me.

Meeting the Dead

If we've loved them, it's what we want, and sometimes
Wanting works. With my father it happened driving
From Santa Monica to Pasadena

A night of a full moon, the freeway wide
Open, the palm trees black. I was recalling
How for two years after that shy man's death
I thought only of death, how in April weather
I used to lock the Volkswagen windows so nothing
Pleasant or fragrant would reach me, how one time
I saw him staring in a ladies' room
Mirror, and stood in my tracks, paralyzed,
He looked so bitter, until his face dissolved
Back into my face. . . . My radio was playing
The usual late-night jazz. No other cars
Drove with me on the freeway. I hated it
That we would never meet in mutual old
Age to drink a beer—it was all he ever
Drank—and declare our love, the way I'd planned
All through high school, picturing us in
A sunny doorway facing a back garden;
Something out of a book. I hated it
That I was pushing forty and could still
Curl like a snail, a fetus, weeping for him.
While I was feeling that, the next things happened
All at once, like iron slugs
Being pulled into a magnet.
This has been *mourning*, I thought; then a sound came,
Like a door clicking closed, and I understood
Right off that I was finished, that I would
Never feel any more grief for him—
And at the same time, he was present; had been,
I now saw, all along, for these twelve years,
Waiting for me to finish my mourning.
At that I had to laugh, and he swiftly slipped
From outside the Buick, where he had been floating.
He was just in me. His round eyesockets
Were inside mine, his shoulderblades aligned
With my own, his right foot and right palm
Lay with mine on the gas pedal and steering wheel—
A treat for him, who'd never learned to drive.
The San Gabriel foothills were approaching
Like parents, saying here's a friend for life,
And then they blocked the moon, and I was back
On suburb streets, quietly passing
Orderly gardens and one-storied homes.

Years

for J.P.O.

I have wished you dead and myself dead,
How could it be otherwise.

I have broken into you like a burglar
And you've set your dogs on me.
You have been a hurricane to me
And a pile of broken sticks
A child could kick.
I have climbed you like a monument, gasping,
For the exercise and the view,
And leaned over the railing at the top—
Strong and warm, that summer wind.

Linda Pastan

To a Daughter Leaving Home

When I taught you
at eight to ride
a bicycle, loping along
beside you
as you wobbled away
on two round wheels,
my own mouth rounding
in surprise when you pulled
ahead down the curved
path of the park,
I kept waiting
for the thud
of your crash as I
sprinted to catch up,
while you grew
smaller, more breakable
with distance,
pumping, pumping
for your life, screaming
with laughter,
the hair flapping
behind you like a
handkerchief waving
goodbye.

I Think Table

> I think table and I say chair. . . .
> Gloria Fuertes

I think table,
and I say chair.
I walk into the kitchen
for a bottle of cold milk,
but when I walk out
my hands are filled

with warm bread.
Everything I know
I begin to forget, starting
with the names of brothers
and sons. Soon I will be back
in the alleys of childhood,
reaching for a hand
that by now is bone.
The days grow colder.
I sort through the shadows
as if they were old photographs,
and under my gaze
the aging eskimo left
on the mountain fades
into pure parable.
And facts continue
to detach themselves, one by one
like loose buttons,
while the tea steeps
in its chipped pot,
bitter and consoling
as the memory of the table
at which we ate together,
your casual arm
on the back of my chair.

The Animals

When I see a suckling pig turn
on the spit, its mouth around
an apple, or feel the soft
muzzle of a horse
eating a windfall from my hand,
I think about the animals
when Eden closed down,
who stole no fruit themselves.

After feeding so long
from Adam's outstretched hand
and sleeping under the mild stars,
flank to flank,
what did they do on freezing nights?
Still ignorant of nests and lairs
did they try to warm themselves
at the fiery leaves of the first autumn?

And how did they learn to sharpen
fangs and claws? Who taught them
the first lesson: that flesh

had been transformed to meat?
Tiger and Bear. Elk and Dove.
God saved them places on the Ark,
and Christ would honor them with
parables, calling himself the Lamb of God.

We train our dogs in strict obedience
at which we failed ourselves.
But sometimes the sound of barking
fills the night like distant artillery,
a sound as chilling as the bellow
of steers led up the ramps
of cattle cars whose gates swing
shut on them, as Eden's did.

Marge Piercy

My mother's body

1

The dark socket of the year
the pit, the cave where the sun lies down
and threatens never to rise,
when despair descends softly as the snow
covering all paths and choking roads:

then hawk-faced pain seized you
threw you so you fell with a sharp
cry, a knife tearing a bolt of silk.
My father heard the crash but paid
no mind, napping after lunch,

yet fifteen hundred miles north
I heard and dropped a dish.
Your pain sunk talons in my skull
and crouched there cawing, heavy
as a great vessel filled with water,

oil or blood, till suddenly next day
the weight lifted and I knew your mind
had guttered out like the Chanukah
candles that burn so fast, weeping
veils of wax down the chanukiyot.

Those candles were laid out,
friends invited, ingredients bought
for latkes and apple pancakes,
that holiday for liberation
and the winter solstice

when tops turn like little planets.
Shall you have all or nothing
take half or pass by untouched?
Nothing you got, *Nun* said the dreidl
as the room stopped spinning.

The angel folded you up like laundry
your body thin as an empty dress.
Your clothes were curtains
hanging on the window of what had
been your flesh and now was glass.

Outside in Florida shopping plazas

186

loudspeakers blared Christmas carols
and palm trees were decked with blinking
lights. Except by the tourist
hotels, the beaches were empty.

Pelicans with pregnant pouches
flapped overhead like pterodactyls.
In my mind I felt you die.
First the pain lifted and then
you flickered and went out.

2
I walk through the rooms of memory.
Sometimes everything is shrouded in dropcloths,
every chair ghostly and muted.

Other times memory lights up from within
bustling scenes acted just the other side
of a scrim through which surely I could reach

my fingers tearing at the flimsy curtain
of time which is and isn't and will be
the stuff of which we're made and unmade.

In sleep the other night I met you, seventeen,
your first nasty marriage just annulled,
thin from your abortion, clutching a book

against your cheek and trying to look
older, trying to look middle class,
trying for a job at Wanamaker's,

dressing for parties in cast-off
stage costumes of your sisters'. Your eyes
were hazy with dreams. You did not

notice me waving as you wandered
past and I saw your slip was showing.
You stood still while I fixed your clothes,

as if I were your mother. Remember me
combing your springy black hair, ringlets
that seemed metallic, glittering;

remember me dressing you, my seventy-year-
old mother who was my last doll baby,
giving you too late what your youth had wanted.

3
What is this mask of skin we wear,
what is this dress of flesh,
this coat of few colors and little hair?

This voluptuous seething heap of desires
and fears, squeaking mice turned up
in a steaming haystack with their babies?

This coat has been handed down, an heirloom,
this coat of black hair and ample flesh,

this coat of pale slightly ruddy skin.

This set of hips and thighs, these buttocks,
they provided cushioning for my grandmother
Hannah, for my mother Bert and for me

and we all sat on them in turn, those major
muscles on which we walk and walk and walk
over the earth in search of peace and plenty.

My mother is my mirror and I am hers.
What do we see? Our face grown young again,
our breasts grown firm, legs lean and elegant.

Our arms quivering with fat, eyes
set in the bark of wrinkles, hands puffy,
our belly seamed with childbearing.

Give me your dress so I can try it on.
Oh it will not fit you, Mother, you are too fat.
I will not fit you, Mother.

I will not be the bride you can dress,
the obedient dutiful daughter you would chew,
a dog's leather bone to sharpen your teeth.

You strike me sometimes just to hear the sound.
Loneliness turns your fingers into hooks
barbed and drawing blood with their caress.

My twin, my sister, my lost love,
I carry you in me like an embryo
as once you carried me.

4
What is it we turn from, what is it we fear?
Did I truly think you could put me back inside?
Did I think I would fall into you as into a molten
furnace and be recast, that I would become you?

What did you fear in me, the child who wore
your hair, the woman who let that black hair
grow long as a banner of darkness, when you
a proper flapper wore yours cropped?

You pushed and you pulled on my rubbery
flesh, you kneaded me like a ball of dough.
Rise, rise, and then you pounded me flat.
Secretly the bones formed in the bread.

I became willful, private as a cat.
You never knew what alleys I had wandered.
You called me bad and I posed like a gutter
queen in a dress sewn of knives.

All I feared was being stuck in a box
with a lid. A good woman appeared to me
indistinguishable from a dead one
except that she worked all the time.

188

Your payday never came. Your dreams ran
with bright colors like Mexican cottons
that bled onto the drab sheets of the day
and would not bleach with scrubbing.

My dear, what you said was one thing
but what you sang was another, sweetly
subversive and dark as blackberries,
and I became the daughter of your dream.

This body is your body, ashes now
and roses, but alive in my eyes, my breasts,
my throat, my thighs. You run in me
a tang of salt in the creek waters of my blood,

you sing in my mind like wine. What you
did not dare in your life you dare in mine.

Something to look forward to

Menopause—word used as an insult:
a menopausal woman, mind or poem
as if not to leak regularly or on the caprice
of the moon, the collision of egg and sperm,
were the curse we first learned to call that blood.

I have twisted myself to praise that bright splash.
When my womb opens its lips on the full
or dark of the moon, that connection
aligns me as it does the sea. I quiver,
a compass needle thrilling with magnetism.

Yet for every celebration there's the time
it starts on a jet with the seatbelt sign on.
Consider the trail of red amoebae
crawling onto hostess's sheets to signal
my body's disregard of calendar, clock.

How often halfway up the side of a mountain,
during a demonstration with the tactical police
force drawn up in tanks between me and a toilet;
during an endless wind machine panel with four males
I the token woman and they with iron bladders,

I have felt that wetness and wanted to strangle
my womb like a mouse. Sometimes it feels cosmic
and sometimes it feels like mud. Yes, I have prayed
to my blood on my knees in toilet stalls
simply to show its rainbow of deliverance.

My friend Penny at twelve, being handed a napkin
the size of an ironing board cover, cried out

Do I have to do this from now till I die?
No, said her mother, it stops in middle age.
Good, said Penny, there's something to look forward to.

Today supine, groaning with demon crab claws
gouging my belly, I tell you I will secretly dance
and pour out a cup of wine on the earth
when time stops that leak permanently;
I will burn my last tampons as votive candles.

Joy Road and Livernois

My name was Pat. We used to read Poe in bed
till we heard blood dripping in the closet.
I fell in love with a woman who could ring
all bells of my bones tolling, jangling.
But she in her cape and her Caddy
had to shine in the eyes of the other pimps,
a man among monkeys, so she turned me on the streets
to strut my meek ass. To quiet my wailing
she taught me to slip the fire in my arm,
the white thunder rolling over till nothing
hurt but coming down. One day I didn't.
I was fifteen. My face gleamed in the casket.

My name was Evie. We used to shoplift,
my giggling, wide-eyed questions, your fast hands;
we picked up boys together on the corners.
The cops busted me for stealing, milled me,
sent me up for prostitution because I weren't
no virgin. I met my boyfriend in the courts.
Together we robbed a liquor store that wouldn't
sell us whiskey. I liked to tote a gun.
It was the cleanest thing I ever held.
It was the only power I ever had.
I could look any creep straight on in the eyes.
A state trooper blew my face off in Marquette.

My name was Peggy. Across the street from the gas-
works, my mom raised nine kids. My brother
in law porked me while my sister gave birth
choking me with the pillow when I screamed.
I got used to it. My third boyfriend knocked me up.
Now I've been pregnant for twenty years,
always a belly bigger than me to push around
like an overloaded wheelbarrow ready to spill
on the blacktop. Now it's my last one,
a tumor big as a baby when they found it.
When I look in the mirror I see my mom.

Remember how we braided each other's hair,
mine red, yours black. Now I'm bald
as an egg and nearly boiled through.

I was Teresa. I used to carry a long clasp
knife I stole from my uncle. Running nights
through the twitching streets, I'd finger it.
It made me feel as mean as any man.
My boyfriend worked on cars until they flew.
All those hot nights riding around and around
when we had noplace to go but back.
Those hot nights we raced out on the highway
faster faster till the blood fizzed in my throat
like shaken soda. It shot in an arc
when he hit the pole and I went out the windshield,
the knife I showed you how to use, still
on its leather thong between my breasts
where it didn't save me from being cut in two.

I was Gladys. Like you, I stayed in school.
I did not lay down in back seats with boys.
I became a nurse, married, had three sons.
My ankles swelled. I worked the night hours
among the dying and accident cases. My husband
left me for a girl he met in a bar, left debts,
a five-year-old Chevy, a mortgage.
My oldest came home in a body bag. My youngest
ran off. The middle one drinks beer and watches
the soaps since the Kelsey-Hayes plant closed.
Then my boy began to call me from the alley.
Every night he was out there calling, Mama,
help me! It hurts, Mama! Take me home.
This is the locked ward and the drugs
eat out my head like busy worms.

With each of them I lay down, my twelve
year old scrawny tough body like weathered
wood pressed to their pain, and we taught
each other love and pleasure and ourselves.
We invented the places, the sounds, the smells,
the little names. At twelve I was violent
in love, a fiery rat, a whip snake,
a starving weasel, all teeth and speed
except for the sore fruit of my new breasts
pushing out. What did I learn? To value
my pleasure and how little the love of women
can shield against the acid city rain.

You surge among my many ghosts. I never think
I got out because I was smart, brave, hard-
working, attractive. Evie was brave.
Gladys and Teresa were smart. Peggy worked
sixteen hours. Pat gleamed like olivewood
polished to a burnish as if fire lived in wood.
I wriggled through an opening left just big enough

191

for one. There is no virtue in survival
only luck, and a streak of indifference
that I could take off and keep going.

I got out of those Detroit blocks where the air
eats stone and melts flesh, where jobs
dangle and you jump and jump, where there are
more drugs than books, more ways to die
than ways to live, because I ran fast,
ran hard, and never stopped looking back.
It is not looking back that turned me
to salt, no, I taste my salt from the mines
under Detroit, the salt of our common juices.
Girls who lacked everything except trouble,
contempt and rough times, girls
used like urinals, you are the salt
keeps me from rotting as the years swell.
I am the fast train you are travelling in
to a world of a different color, and the love
we cupped so clumsily in our hands to catch
rages and drives onward, an engine of light.

Margaret Randall

Immigration Law

When I ask the experts
"how much time do I have?"
I don't want an answer in years
or arguments.

I must know if there are hours enough
to mend this relationship,
see a book all the way to its birthing,
stand beside my father
on his journey.

I want to know how many seasons of chamisa
will be yellow then grey-green
and yellow
         /light/
               again,
how many red cactus flowers
will bloom beside my door.

I do not want to follow language
like a dog with its tail between its legs.

I need time equated with music,
hours rising in bread,
years deep from connections.

The present always holds a tremor of the past.

Give me a handful of future
to rub against my lips.

Talk to Me

Talk to me. Three
words
moving with heavy feet
across the open spaces.

A signal,
or the beginning of a poem.

Talk to me. Not meaning
"how are things going?" Not meaning
"they *can't* do this to you"
(they can, they are)
not even
"what can I do to help?"

Do it, that's all.
Please.
No more questions, no more
knowledgeable statements.

Three words. Begin a poem. Take your life
and use it.

Under Attack

for Marian McDonald

Listen. These voices are under attack.

Ismaela of the dark tobacco house. Grandma.
A maid her lifetime of winters, granddaughter
of slaves.
Straight to my eyes:
"My mama used to tell me, one of these days
the hens gonna shit upwards!
And I'd stare at those hens' asses, wondering
when will that happen?
When we pushed the big ones down
and pulled the little ones up!"

"For Mama, Papa, and Blackie" she wrote
on the poem she left to say goodbye.
Nicaragua, 1977.
Disappear
or be disappeared.
Dora Maria whose gaze
her mother always knew. She trembled
at her first delivery,
took a city fearlessly.

Rain and the river rising. Catalina
chases her ducks
that stray.
"And my months," she cries,
on the platform with poles. A house
to do over. "My months
gone in the hospital at Iquitos

and the full moon
bringing a madness to my head."
Her body is light against my touch.
A woman's voice, parting
such density of rain.

Xuan, my cold hand in hers,
evokes the barracks.
"Soldiers who were our brothers.
Night after night, village by village.
Quang Tri, 1974.
Gunfire
replaced by quiet conversation.
The work of women.
Xuan's history, too, is under attack.

Dominga takes her memory down
from the needle trade, Don Pedro,
her own babies
dead from hunger.
"I want to tell you my story, leave it
to the young ones
so they'll know."
We are rocking. We are laughing.
This woman who rescued the flag at Ponce
Puerto Rico, 1938.
Known by that act alone.
Until a book
carries her words. Her voice.

I bring you these women.
Listen.
They speak, but their lives
are under attack.

They too are denied adjustment of status
in the land of the free. In the home of the brave.

Adrienne Rich

Yom Kippur 1984

> I drew solitude over me, on the long shore.
> Robinson Jeffers, **Prelude**

> For whoever does not afflict his soul throughout
> this day, shall be cut off from his people.
> **Leviticus 23:29**

What is a Jew in solitude?
What would it mean not to feel lonely or afraid
far from your own or those you have called your own?
What is a woman in solitude: a queer woman or man?
In the empty street, on the empty beach, in the desert
what in this world as it is can solitude mean?

The glassy, concrete octagon suspended from the cliffs
with its electric gate, its perfected privacy
is not what I mean
the pick-up with a gun parked at a turn-out in Utah or the
                       Golan Heights
is not what I mean
the poet's tower facing the western ocean, acres of forest
                   planted to the east, the woman reading in the
                   cabin, her attack dog suddenly risen
is not what I mean

Three thousand miles from what I once called home
I open a book searching for some lines I remember
about flowers, something to bind me to this coast as lilacs
                   in the dooryard once
bound me back there—yes, lupines on a burnt mountainside,
something that bloomed and faded and was written down
in the poet's book, forever:
Opening the poet's book
I find the hatred in the poet's heart: . . . *the hateful-eyed*
and human-bodied are all about me: you that love multitude
            may have them

Robinson Jeffers, multitude
is the blur flung by distinct forms against these landward
            valleys
and the farms that run down to the sea; the lupines
are multitude, and the torched poppies, the grey Pacific
            unrolling its scrolls of surf,
and the separate persons, stooped

over sewing machines in denim dust, bent under the shattering
        skies of harvest
who sleep by shifts in never-empty beds have their various
                                            dreams
Hands that pick, pack, steam, stitch, strip, stuff, shell, scrape,
        scour, belong to a brain like no other
Must I argue the love of multitude in the blur or defend
a solitude of barbed-wire and searchlights, the survivalist's
        final solution, have I a choice?

To wander far from your own or those you have called your own
to hear strangeness calling you from far away
and walk in that direction, long and far, not calculating risk
to go to meet the Stranger without fear or weapon, protection
        nowhere on your mind?
the Jew on the icy, rutted road on Christmas Eve prays for
        another Jew
the woman in the ungainly twisting shadows of the street: *Make
        those be a woman's footsteps:* (as if she could believe
        in a woman's god)

Find someone like yourself. Find others.
Agree you will never desert each other.
Understand that any rift among you
means power to those who want to do you in.
Close to the center, safety; toward the edges, danger.
But I have a nightmare to tell: I am trying to say
that to be with my people is my dearest wish
but that I also love strangers
that I crave separateness
I hear myself stuttering these words
to my worst friends and my best enemies
who watch for my mistakes in grammar
my mistakes in love.
This is the day of atonement; but do my people forgive me?
If a cloud knew loneliness and fear, I would be that cloud.

To love the Stranger, to love solitude—am I writing merely
        about privilege
about drifting from the center, drawn to edges,
a privilege we can't afford in the world that is,
who are hated as being of our kind: faggot kicked into the icy
        river, woman dragged from her stalled car
into the mist-struck mountains, used and hacked to death
young scholar shot at the university gates on a summer evening
        walk, his prizes and studies nothing, nothing
        availing his Blackness
Jew deluded that she's escaped the tribe, the laws of her
                                            exclusion,
        the men too holy to touch her hand; Jew who has turned
        her back
on *midrash* and *mitzvah* (yet wears the *chai* on a thong between her
        breasts) hiking alone

found with a swastika carved in her back at the foot of the cliffs
        (did she die as queer or as Jew?)

Solitude, O taboo, endangered species
on the mist-struck spur of the mountain, I want a gun to defend
                                                                you
In the desert, on the deserted street, I want what I can't have:
your elder sister, Justice, her great peasant's hand outspread
her eye, half-hooded, sharp and true
And I ask myself, have I thrown courage away?
have I traded off something I don't name?
To what extreme will I go to meet the extremist?
What will I do to defend my want or anyone's want to search
        for her spirit-vision
far from the protection of those she has called her own?
Will I find O solitude
your plumes, your breasts, your hair
against my face, as in childhood, your voice like the mocking-
                                                            bird's
singing *Yes, you are loved, why else this song?*
in the old places, anywhere?

What is a Jew in solitude?
What is a woman in solitude, a queer woman or man?
When the winter flood-tides wrench the tower from the rock,
        crumble the prophet's headland, and the farms slide
            into the sea
when leviathan is endangered and Jonah becomes revenger
when center and edges are crushed together, the extremities
        crushed together on which the world was founded
when our souls crash together, Arab and Jew, howling our
        loneliness within the tribes
when the refugee child and the exile's child re-open the
        blasted and forbidden city
when we who refuse to be women and men as women and men
                                                            are
        chartered, tell our stories of solitude spent in
        multitude
in that world as it may be, newborn and haunted, what will
        solitude mean?

from Contradictions: Tracking Poems

2
Heart of cold.   Bones of cold.   Scalp of cold.
the grey   the black   the blond   the red
hairs on a skull of cold.   Within that skull
the thought of war   the sovereign thought
the coldest of all thought.   Dreaming shut down
everything kneeling down to cold   intelligence

smirking with cold   memory
squashed and frozen cold   breath
half held-in for cold.   The freezing people
of a freezing nation   eating
luxury food or garbage
frozen tongues licking the luxury meat
or the pizza-crust   the frozen eyes
welded to other eyes   also frozen
the cold hands trying to stroke   the coldest sex.
Heart of cold   Sex of cold   Intelligence of cold
My country   wedged fast in history
stuck in the ice

3

My mouth hovers across your breasts
in the short grey winter afternoon
in this bed   we are delicate
and tough   so hot with joy we amaze ourselves
tough   and delicate   we play rings
around each other   our daytime candle burns
with its peculiar light   and if the snow
begins to fall outside   filling the branches
and if the night falls   without announcement
these are the pleasures of winter
sudden, wild and delicate   your fingers
exact   my tongue exact at the same moment
stopping to laugh at a joke
my love   hot on your scent   on the cusp of winter

4

He slammed his hand across my face   and I
let him do that until   I stopped letting him do it
so I'm in for life.

. . . . He kept saying I was crazy, he'd lock me up
until I went to Women's Lib and they
told me he'd been abusing me as much
as if he'd hit me: emotional abuse.
They told me how to answer back.   That I could
answer back.   But my brother-in-law's a shrink
with the State. I have to watch my step.
If I stay just within bounds they can't come and get me.
Women's Lib taught me the words to say
to remind myself and him I'm a person with rights
like anyone.   But answering back's no answer.

5

She is carrying my madness   and I dread her
avoid her when I can
She walks along I.S. 93   howling
in her bare feet
She is number 6375411
in a cellblock in Arkansas
and I dread what she is paying for   that is mine
She has fallen asleep at last in the battered

199

women's safe-house   and I dread
her dreams   that I also dream
If never I become exposed or confined like this
what am I hiding
O sister of nausea   of broken ribs   of isolation
what is this freedom I protect   how is it mine

11
I came out of the hospital like a woman
who'd watched a massacre
not knowing how to tell
my adhesions   the lingering infections
from the pain on the streets
In my room on Yom Kippur they took me off
                                        morphine
I saw shadows on the wall   the dying and the dead
They said Christian Phalangists did it
then Kol Nidre on the radio   and my own
unhoused spirit   trying to find a home
Was it then or another day
in what order did it happen
I thought   *They call this elective surgery*
but we all have died of this.

20
The tobacco fields lie fallow   the migrant pickers
no longer visible here
where undocumented intelligences travailed
on earth they had no stake in
though the dark leaves growing beneath white veils
were beautiful   and the barns opened out like fans
All this of course could have been done differently
This valley itself: one more contradiction
the paradise fields   the brute skyscrapers
the pesticidal wells

I have been wanting for years
to write a poem   equal to these
material forces
and I have always failed
I wasn't looking for a muse
only a reader by whom   I could not be mistaken

22
In a bald skull sits our friend,   in a helmet
of third-degree burns
her quizzical melancholy grace
her irreplaceable self   in utter peril
In the radioactive desert walks a woman
in a black dress   white-haired   steady
as a luminous hand of a clock
in circles she walks   knitting
and unknitting her scabbed fingers
Her face is expressionless   shall we pray to her
shall we speak of the loose pine-needles   how they shook

200

like the pith of country summers
from the sacks of pitchblende ore in the tin-roofed
shack
where it all began
Shall we accuse her of denial
first of the self   then of the mixed virtue
of the purest science   shall we be wise for her
in hindsight   shall we scream *It has come to this*
Shall we praise her   shall we let her wander
the atomic desert   in peace?

Upcountry

The silver shadow   where the line falls grey
and pearly   the unborn villages quivering
under the rock   the snail   traveling the crevice
the furred, flying white insect like a tiny
intelligence lacing the air
this woman whose lips lie parted
after long speech
her white hair unrestrained

All that you never paid
or have with difficulty paid
attention to

Change and be forgiven!   the roots of the forest
muttered   but you tramped through   guilty
unable to take forgiveness   neither do you
give mercy

She is asleep now   dangerous   her mind
slits the air like silk   travels faster than sound
like scissors flung into the next century

Even as you watch for the trout's hooked stagger
across the lake   the crack of light and the crumpling bear
her mind was on them first
when forgiveness ends
her love means danger

When/Then

Tell us
        how we'll be together   in that time

patch of sun on a gritty floor; an old newspaper, torn
for toilet paper and coughed-up scum   Don't talk, she said

when we still love but are no longer young

they bring you a raw purple stick and say
it is one of her fingers;   it could be
                         Tell us

about aging, what it costs, how women
have loved forty, fifty years
                  enamel basin, scraped
down to the bare iron   some ashen hairs   red fluid
they say is her blood   how can you

Tell us about the gardens we will keep, the milk
we'll drink from our own goats
                    she needs
anti-biotics they say which will be given
when you name names   they show you her fever chart

Tell us about community   the joy
of coming to rest
          among women
                who will love us

you choose between your community
and her   later others
will come through the cell   not all of them will love you
whichever way you choose

Don't talk, she said   (you will learn to hear
only her voice when they close in on you)   Don't talk

Why are you telling us this?
                patch of sun on a gritty
floor, bad dreams, a torn newspaper, someone's blood
in a scraped basin. . . .

Ruthann Robson

Regine's Rebuke to Kierkegaard

                    The years
flew by like magpies trailing bright
ribbons through the twilight. I
have fourteen sons. Not even one is
named Søren. Their eyelashes curl
dark and thick as the tails of Danish ducks
in winter. Some of my boys have handsome
fathers. Do not worry, my jejune darling, you
are not being charged with paternity.

                    The nights
I seduced you under my red coverlets
produced nothing; only your extravagant
guilt about acquiring a few basic skills.
It was distressingly easy to feign innocence.
The blood was a chicken's. I would blow
out the flickering romance of the candle and laugh
at you under my breath. Afterwards,
you would beseech God with your boring sins.

                    The morning
you decided you were too god-like to marry,
we sat on a hill round as my breast. The park
was fertile with spring and made me think
of all the places you had never kissed.
At that moment, you were more serious, more
tormented, more interestingly blond, than anyone
I ever knew, but your words were dishonest as parrots
caged as pets. I stilled the wings of my banter.

                    The day
you first touched me, you had taken me to
a museum in the city. One of us was explaining
the paintings of dead men, while the other choked
on the stale air. The halls were narrow as children's
coffins. As your fingers traced the braid round
the nape of my neck, I lifted my skirt to avoid
the curse of lust in a public place. Even then,
you did not guess I wore the feathers of a gypsy.

                    The future
you envisioned for me was bleak, but less
so than yours. Without crystal or leaves,

you foresaw my fatal flaw: the capacity to be happy.
You wasted your wind berating me. You
were fearful and trembling and sicker than death.

Your tragedy
was that you deflected your agony with eloquent
edifices, built to explain why you gave me up
when I was never yours to give.
My tragedy
was that your buildings were so expertly
mirrored, my messages died on carrier pigeons
crashing into images of boundless sky.

the consort

for larkin

1
all romance is a parody of this:
child
& woman as Madonna/Goddess

the day you learned to kiss:
the sweet smell of my breast
on your excited wet breath

your giggles like blue baubles
for a sapphire necklace

more precious than precious

2
when i was engaged
i stole my mother's pearls
& hocked them
to pay for an abortion
for my lover's lover

then I eloped
alone
with you in my womb

& we gave birth
alone
in a room at The Desert Inn

3
that a winter night
the stars brightly gossiping
& the moon
a bastard itself
almost full & approving

the cord was cut
by a butcher's knife

no doctor stitched me shut

there are scars
that are not meant to be
completely healed

4
no one needs to tell me
this is forbidden
:in bed together
sleeping through night after
cold night after hot night

our scent is so mingled
no animal could distinguish
between us

or would need to

5
i know how
Mary believed herself a virgin

never have i been purer
                less subjugated
                more sensuous

sweet sweet Jesus

something bares its teeth
& howls
in the desert

6
your mouth a telescope
focused on my left nipple
: your favorite
like an actress
drawing on the morning's
first cigarette
your pull is long & lusty
my right breast tingles
jealously & sprays milk
with the sloppy beauty
of an extravagant gift

7
i read you ancient
tragedies
from a leather bound set
that was a present
from someone's father

the other daughter
got a diamond pendant

that slit her throat

we are a chorus
& pass judgment
on everyone

8
your need is large & purple
as Jupiter
& calls my name
sharply lacking syllables

i rock you back to sleep
& leave you
alone on our bed
buoyed by a small sea of blue
pillows

& you dream orbits
that are complete
without me

9
i am a ruby planet
of ambition
for you

lawyer/doctor/actor
millionaire/jeweler/savior
:nothing is good enough

except author
i want you to write a new plot
for Orestes
for Oedipus
do not have the son commit Clytemnestra's murder
do not have the son seduce Jocasta's suicide

you are the only
predator who can destroy only
one of us

Wendy Rose

To the Vision-Seekers: Remember This

you star-fliers, you galaxy-dangers,
where do you think you got the flesh
with which to name the bend of your symbols?
That math you paint on the black walls of classrooms—
the furious way you shout calculations—
how you point and scratch and erase and wonder;
how got the dreamer her dreams,
the hunter her arrows, the doctor her way
to plant and pray, the priest proper songs
for sunrise, the sick?
Where grew the hand
to guide infant trails,
the straight-sculpted cliffs
against which we stand,
brown feet balanced on cedar bark shreds,
and—wet with the yellow mist of babyhood—
where did you learn to walk
to your visions?

> The soot-stained knees you touch
> are those of Clay Mother among her pots,
> of Granite Rock Woman holding the sand
> and agate on beaches and hills,
>
> the one with the melon breast
> who waters each harvest,
> and she who with sharpened sticks
> sings seed into the soil,
>
> Sunrise Singer with her drum-steady voice
> who explains and explains,
> Spider Grandmother whose rough round
> and brown hands will take us
>
> to her own guiding moon, her stolen fire,
> in a summer-dry starship
> or a single drop of water,
> a day immense with rain
>
> or a night of falling feathers.
> Women all women where you come from.
> As you are flying, Earth is the one
> to remember.

Coming of Age in "The Movement"

Howard slapped the man next to him on the shoulder
and walked up belly out like he was commissioner
and I believe he might have been, he was ambitious
and big, for sure one of those Arikaras
like a buffalo or a mountain from head to hip
and from there on down a small tree

and I was so young
when he asked for strands of my hair,
pieces of my teeth, nail clippings, and rolled them
up in a twine ball, said I should kneel before him
and spread sage tea on his feet—I remember
he said he was Jesus now red and I had so recently
been Catholic I believed him for I needed him
Oh Jesus, come back Arikara, big and red,
and could it be I was the harlot he would save
from a stoning—he said my mouth
was full of strawberries and he was a hummingbird
come to taste with his delicate tongue.
Oh I was barely a woman in those days
and he was almost my father's age.

I am grown up, Howard, you know
and there is a difference between
to be settled like the striking of earth
by falling stars or the great blaze
of our victories, the neon pigment
of our scars. I planted four songs
for you to remember me by
as you planted your tree; red on red
I was the forest you entered,
your drum dragging silent behind you.
Every dance we did
is swirling between my knees,
slow southern steps, drums but echoes,
movement made into prayer,
memory made of smoke.
I am not the shy girl I was;
I am not the harlot nor the messenger
nor the disciple nor the goddess,
none of the things you said, not even
strawberries. I am a woman,
an Indian woman, a Breed, one whose shawl
contains the face of the sun,
one whose hand brews peppermint tea,
dips to the drybread in the skillet.
I am a woman who stands strong
in the distant music and the wind;
I am a woman with voices in my hair.
I am a woman retreating
through the silent door, the sleeping cat,
the morning free of terror.

Comment on Ethnopoetics and Literacy

While traveling with Ohnainewk, I remarked, as best I could in Eskimo, "The wind is cold." He laughed. "How", he asked, "can the *wind* be cold? You're cold; you're unhappy. But the wind isn't cold or unhappy."

Edmund Carpenter, anthropologist

I gradually came to understand that the marks on the pages were trapped words. Anyone could learn to decipher the symbols and turn the trapped words loose again into speech. The ink of the print trapped the thoughts; they could no more get away than a *doomboo* could get out of a pit!

Modupe, an African native

Pick the words
from the evening rain
with throats exposed,
bound and thrown, quickly
thrust the spike
in bladeside down
and turn, now pull it
from the neck
and drain them all
side by side,
guts on the ground,
paws in a small pile,
everything severed
and stripped down
to bone.

Re-make the bodies
in different positions:
this one running, this one alert,
another with one forefoot lifted;
strengthen those dead bones with sticks,
puff out that hanging skin with cotton,
make the muscles bunch again with clay.
Where once they scanned the sky
or the ground for hawk shadows
put tiny glass balls or bits of amber.
Admire what you have done.

Re-arrange the figures
into a natural scene;
paint the background
into jungle or desert,
scatter sand
around their claws.
Remember
how you danced to their beauty,
how you caught your breath watching them run,
how you moved your head listening to them
call to each other,
mating in the moonlight.

You make them move
with the tips of your finger.
You pretend that now
they will live forever.

Weaponry

> This fever dances
> in dead roots?

Are we, then, above ground
to dry out, exposed, turning
upside down and blowing away
in the hot wind of summer?

> Bow and arrow / mouth and tongue
> curve; this song is all,
> disguised

and do you see
the redwood in there,
the sweet firm
dogwood blossom,
the eagle
slowly tipping
above?

We are surrounded by the bees
and burned holy in their song
as they take us to feed
from the nectar on their legs
and fed like that we are fertile
and gather ourselves
like the sea gathers clouds
and then bumps on the trail
as a travois bumps to where
the roots
thirst.

Sonia Sanchez

Poem Written After Reading Wright's "American Hunger"

for the homegirl who told Wright of her desire to go to the circus

such a simple desire
wanting to go to the circus
wanting to see the animals
orange with laughter.

such a simple need
amid yo/easy desire
to ride her
while clowns waited offstage
and children tugged at her young legs.

did you tell her man that we're
all acrobats tumbling out of
our separate arenas?
you peeling her
skin while dreams turned
somersaults in her eyes.

such a simple woman
illiterate with juices
in a city where hunger
is passed around for seconds.

Present

This woman vomiting her
hunger over the world
this melancholy woman forgotten
before memory came
this yellow movement bursting forth like
coltrane's melodies all mouth
buttocks moving like palm trees,
this honeycoatedalabamianwoman
raining rhythm of blue/black/smiles
this yellow woman carrying beneath her breasts

pleasures without tongues
this woman whose body weaves
desert patterns,
this woman, wet with wandering,
reviving the beauty of forests and winds
is telling you secrets
gather up your odors and listen
as she sings the mold from memory.

        there is no place
for a soft/black/woman.
there is no smile green enough or
summertime words warm enough to allow my growth.
and in my head
i see my history
standing like a shy child
and i chant lullabies
as i ride my past on horseback
tasting the thirst of yesterday tribes
hearing the ancient/black/woman
me, singing   hay-hay-hay-hay-ya-ya-ya.
                         hay-hay-hay-hay-ya-ha-ya.
like a slow scent
beneath the sun
        and i dance my
creation and my grandmothers gathering
from my bones like great wooden birds
spread their wings
while their long/legged/laughter
stretches the night.
        and i taste the
seasons of my birth. mangoes. papayas.
drink my woman/coconut/milks
stalk the ancient grandfathers
sipping on proud afternoons
walk like a song round my waist
tremble like a new/born/child troubled
with new breaths
        and my singing
becomes the only sound of a
blue/black/magical/woman. walking.
womb ripe. walking. loud with mornings. walking.
making pilgrimage to herself. walking.

Kwa mama zetu waliotuzaa*

death is a five o'clock door forever changing time.
    and it was morning without sun or shadow;

a morning already afternoon. sky. cloudy with incense.
    and it was morning male in speech;
feminine in memory.
but i am speaking of everyday occurrences:
of days unrolling bandages for civilized wounds;
of gaudy women chanting rituals under a waterfall of stars;
of men freezing their sperms in diamond-studded wombs;
of children abandoned to a curfew of marble.

as morning is the same as nite death and life are one.
    spring. settling down on you like
green dust. mother. ambushed by pain in
rooms bloated with a century of cancer.
yo/face a scattered cry from queequeg's wooden bier.
    mother. i call out to you
traveling up the congo. i am preparing a place for you:
        nite made of female rain
        i am ready to sing her song
        prepare a place for her
        she comes to you out of turquoise pain.

        restring her eyes for me
        restring her body for me
        restring her peace for me

    no longer full of pain, may she walk
    bright with orange smiles, may she walk
    as it was long ago, may she walk

    abundant with lightning steps, may she walk
    abundant with green trails, may she walk
    abundant with rainbows, may she walk
    as it was long ago, may she walk

at the center of death is birth.
in those days when amherst fertilized by
black myths, rerouted the nile.
you became the word. (shirley, graham, du bois
        you were the dance
    pyramidal sister.
you told us in what egypt our feet
were chained
you. trained in the world's studio
painted the day with palaces
and before you marched the breath
of our ancestors.
        and yo/laughter passing
through a village of blacks
scattered the dead faces.
        and yo/voice lingering
like a shy goat fed our sad hungers.
and i. what pennsylvania day was i sucking dry
while you stuttering a thousand cries
hung yo/breasts on pagodas?
and i. what dreams had i suspended

above our short order lives
when death showered you with bells.
    call her back for me
    bells. call back this memory
    still fresh with cactus pain.

    call her name again. bells.
    shirley. graham. du bois
    has died in china
    and her death demands a capsizing of tides.
olokun**
    she is passing yo/way while
    pilgrim waves whistle complaints to man
olokun.
    a bearer of roots is walking inside
    of you.
    prepare the morning nets to receive her.

before her peace, i know no thirst because of her
behind her peace, i know beauty because of her
under her peace, i know not fear because of her
over her peace, i am wealthy because of her

death is coming. the whole world hears
the buffalo walk of death passing thru the
archway of new life.

    the day is singing
    the day is singing
    he is singing in the mountains

    the nite is singing
    the nite is singing
    she is singing in the earth

i am circling new boundaries
i have been trailing the ornamental
songs of death (life
a strong pine tree
dancing in the wind

i inhale the ancient black breath
cry for every dying (living
creature

come. let us ascend from the
middle of our breath
sacred rhythms
inhaling peace.

* For our mothers who gave us birth
**Goddess of the sea.

May Sarton

On a Winter Night

On a winter night
I sat alone
In a cold room,
Feeling old, strange
At the year's change,
In fire light.

Last fire of youth,
All brilliance burning,
And my year turning—
One dazzling rush,
Like a wild wish
Or blaze of truth.

First fire of age,
And the soft snow
Of ash below—
For the clean wood
The end was good;
For me, an image.

For then I saw
That fires, not I,
Burn down and die;
That flare of gold
Turns old, turns cold.
Not I. I grow.

Nor old, nor young,
The burning sprite
of my delight,
A salamander
In fires of wonder,
Gives tongue, gives tongue!

My Sisters, O My Sisters

Nous qui voulions poser, image ineffaceable
Comme un delta divin notre main sur le sable
                                    Anna de Noailles

Dorothy Wordsworth, dying, did not want to read,
"I am too busy with my own feelings," she said.

And all women who have wanted to break out
Of the prison of consciousness to sing or shout

Are strange monsters who renounce the treasure
Of their silence for a curious devouring pleasure.

Dickinson, Rossetti, Sappho—they all know it.
Something is lost, strained, unforgiven in the poet.

She abdicates from life or like George Sand
Suffers from the mortality in an immortal hand,

Loves too much, spends a whole life to discover
She was born a good grandmother, not a good lover.

Too powerful for men: Madame de Staël. Too sensitive:
Madame de Sévigné, who burdened where she meant to give.

Delicate as that burden was and so supremely lovely,
It was too heavy for her daughter, much too heavy.

Only when she built inward in a fearful isolation
Did any one succeed or learn to fuse emotion

With thought. Only when she renounced did Emily
Begin in the fierce lonely light to learn to be.

Only in the extremity of spirit and the flesh
And in renouncing passion did Sappho come to bless.

Only in the farewells or in old age does sanity
Shine through the crimson stains of their mortality.

And now we who are writing women and strange monsters
Still search our hearts to find the difficult answers,

Still hope that we may learn to lay our hands
More gently and more subtly on the burning sands.

To be through what we make more simply human,
To come to the deep place where poet becomes woman,

Where nothing has to be renounced or given over
In the pure light that shines out from the lover,

In the warm light that brings forth fruit and flower
And that great sanity, that sun, the feminine power.

The Muse as Medusa

I saw you once, Medusa; we were alone.
I looked you straight in the cold eye, cold.
I was not punished, was not turned to stone—
How to believe the legends I am told?

I came as naked as any little fish,
Prepared to be hooked, gutted, caught;
But I saw you, Medusa, made my wish,
And when I left you I was clothed in thought . . .

Being allowed, perhaps, to swim my way
Through the great deep and on the rising tide,
Flashing wild streams, as free and rich as they,
Though you had power marshaled on your side.

The fish escaped to many a magic reef;
The fish explored many a dangerous sea—
The fish, Medusa, did not come to grief,
But swims still in a fluid mystery.

Forget the image: your silence is my ocean,
And even now it teems with life. You chose
To abdicate by total lack of motion,
But did it work, for nothing really froze?

It is all fluid still, that world of feeling
Where thoughts, those fishes, silent, feed and rove;
And fluid, it is also full of healing,
For love is healing, even rootless love.

I turn your face around! It is my face.
That frozen rage is what I must explore—
Oh secret, self-enclosed, and ravaged place!
This is the gift I thank Medusa for.

The Lady and the Unicorn
The Cluny Tapestries

I am the unicorn and bow my head
You are the lady woven into history
And here forever we are bound in mystery
Our wine, Imagination, and our bread,
And I the unicorn who bows his head.

You are all interwoven in my history
And you and I have been most strangely wed
I am the unicorn and bow my head
And lay my wildness down upon your knee
You are the lady woven into history.

217

And here forever we are sweetly wed
With flowers and rabbits in the tapestry
You are the lady woven into history
Imagination is our bridal bed:
We lie ghostly upon it, no word said.

Among the flowers of the tapestry
I am the unicorn and by your bed
Come gently, gently to bow down my head,
Lay at your side this love, this mystery,
And call you lady of my tapestry.

I am the unicorn and bow my head
To one so sweetly lost, so strangely wed:

You sit forever under a small formal tree
Where I forever search your eyes to be

Rewarded with this shining tragedy
And know your beauty was not cast for me,

Know we are woven all in mystery,
The wound imagined where no one has bled,

My wild love chastened to this history
Where I before your eyes, bow down my head.

Der Abschied

Now frost has broken summer like a glass,
This house and I resume our conversations;
The floors whisper a message as I pass,
I wander up and down these empty rooms
That have become my intimate relations,
Brimmed with your presence where your absence blooms—
And did you come at last, come home, to tell
How all fulfillment tastes of a farewell?

Here is the room where you lay down full length
That whole first day, to read, and hardly stirred,
As if arrival had taken all your strength;
Here is the table where you bent to write
The morning through, and silence spoke its word;
And here beside the fire we talked, as night
Came slowly from the wood across the meadow
To frame half of our brilliant world in shadow.

The rich fulfillment came; we held it all;
Four years of struggle brought us to this season,
Then in one week our summer turned to fall;
The air chilled and we sensed the chill in us,
The passionate journey ending in sweet reason.

The autumn light was there, frost on the grass.
And did you come at last, come home, to tell
How all fulfillment tastes of a farewell?

Departure is the constant at this stage;
And all we know is that we cannot stop,
However much the childish heart may rage.
We are still outward-bound to obligations
And, radiant centers, life must drink us up,
Devour our strength in multiple relations.
Yet I still question in these empty rooms
Brimmed with your presence where your absence blooms,

What stays that can outlast these deprivations?
Now, peopled by the dead, and ourselves dying,
The house and I resume old conversations:
What stays? Perhaps some autumn tenderness,
A different strength that forbids youthful sighing.
Though frost has broken summer like a glass,
Know, as we hear the thudding apples fall,
Not ripeness but the suffering change is all.

Kathleen Spivack

The Servant of Others

At twilight
she is the Servant
of Others, sweeping the stone
hearth and picking cluttered
dishes off the table.
She puts the cat out,
straightens the chairs
in their slant-angles,
tops lamps. Then she
makes bread, covering
the dough in the pans
with a damp cloth and
sets it on a shelf
over the big-clawed stove.
She goes out briefly,
milks Bossie,
and brings the milk
inside, foaming in
buckets; she stirs
butter and cream.

And all the while
she is rocking babies
and turning seams, sewing
the one missing button,
heating water for the
bath and singing. Daisies
and Queen Anne's Lace
vie in a jar on the kitchen
table, soapbubbles in the
sink, and tomato relish,
jewelled in the pantry,
and on the windowsill,
veined pebbles of quartz
and blue glints, chips of
Sandwich glass. She likes

small treasures,
licking them pink
with a rough tongue,
laying out clean linens
and shirts, crisp in their

readiness for bodies.
She is not afraid
to wash anything:
sweet water steams in the
kettle, the flagstone floor
is scrubbd, the bed, its sheets
turned down and waiting.

Now the Servant of Others
sets down her broom and her
sewing and carefully opens
the screen door, slinking out,
moaning gently as she grows
wild fur. She visits
the cow barn, lapping a little milk
and tonguing rats, just playing
with them, in her paws. And then
into the camomile and clover-
quilted fields, cat like.
They lie dark and passive
under the moon as she prowls,
arching her spine, tries out
scratching, flying,
picking up small helpless things
in her claws and carrying them away,
dropping them from great heights
until daybreak, pupils
yellow-ringed and huge,
dilated, hair on end,
screech owl in the hollow
by the frog pond, howling.

West Virginia Handicrafts

From the green woods,
from the flashing wilderness,
she selected one perfect
tree. There she cut her heart,
paring down to the
sap-center, slippery
where the bark peeled back
in three inner layers.
She cut first through
the outer bark,
its rough edges and
satisfactory hurts.
She peeled through the cambium,
cutting the upward life force,

and she went on into the inner
soft grey-brownish scrape
till the delicacy of
white was exposed
like the cry of a woman
during childbirth
that can never be closed.

Then she flayed her name
from the center of hardest
hickory into quarter-inch strips,
using a special flensing knife,
carefully easing herself
at the core, the strips
coming off like apple skin
along the length of the tree.
And she lay herself
in the sun to dry
all one hot day,
entering, that same evening,
a vat of moonshine and
vinegar water
where she rested
for twenty years.

When it was over,
and herself judged fully cured,
she removed herself from the
barrel, strip by
strip. The heartwood
achieved dimensions of softness
as well as flexibility:
the wood was wrinkled
and grey as leather
but it could stretch;
it could turn without groaning:
that cured wood could be shaped.

Then she went on down to the river
and gathered saplings
and bent them, singing
willow willow;
and of her hair
she wove a fern stand,
twisting and plaiting
around a fountain of green
and dampened the fern
each day with river water
from her weeping willow hair:
She could now make anything
with a knife.

And she made of herself
an elegant rocker,
weaving the seat and the

back until she could bear
any kind of weight,
all manner of burdens,
keep secrets,
cradle a child,
wipe away men's tears and never
talk about it,
or sit quietly on porches
and absorb the thoughts of others.

And she set her rocker
next to the fern stand
out in the summer
to watch the trees sway;
she, who once wanted to whittle
a heart, a name, regrets,
even her history,
out of the fierce
undisciplined forest.

The moments-of-past-happiness quilt

This square
is made up of
moments of past happiness
duplicated
throughout the entire quilt
and repeated
in random patterns, no order.
This moments-of-past-happiness quilt
was stitched
by many women, each
in her own bright
kitchen, humming:
different rates of speed. Please
note
the individuality of the
stitching: here
the stitchery is tiny;
some of them
are large and bold.
In parts
the stitches cannot even be seen.
Maybe a certain woman
wasn't happy,
or maybe moments flowed,
one into another, fluidity like sun
so taken for granted we

can't even see her edges.
Over here
the pattern is uneven:
doubt
took hold, uncertainty
and darkness
and a woman faltered.
Moments of perfect happiness
were past
imperfect, could she remember one?
She sat, she didn't get up,
she didn't turn on the lights.
On this blank part
she stitched her name,
too difficult to read—
it's rather like your own. Here,
look at the rainbow center where
the squares converge, the color
of turning prisms. Yet
the center is most
forgettable, somehow. . . .
So many women worked; they blend. . . .
Don't look so hard, my friend.
You will ruin it.
See, it is fading,
it is fading
even while you watch.
Fold the quilt
quickly;
put it away in its box.

A moments-of-past-happiness quilt
is too delicate.
It won't wash.
It won't wear.
It won't do to wrap babies in.
You are lucky to have touched it,
even once.
It cannot be sold;
it does not last.
Do not hope
to use it on your bed.

Anne Stevenson

Attitudes and Beliefs

He sells them puce-painted T-shirts,
  oversized boiler suits,
    lemon tight jeans.

"Beauty?" he says,
  "Let them tell me what beauty is,
    I'll sell it to them."

But you think beauty
  is beauty, the unbuyable heathery
    gap between motorways

over which the kestrel's
  ancient appetite
    hovers, the absolute mercy

of his kill keeping stillness
  in motion, the burrowing vole
    only signifying food.

Or the wind pulling white hairs
  upright out of the ocean,
    exactly as it bullies bolt

upright the hair of this eighty-
  year-old hardly successful artist who,
    upright in the usual gale,

flings wide the car door.
  "If you're going to the station
    of course I'll drive you," while

his wife, adored over fifty years,
  musters in her egg-shaped bohemian basket
    items for contingencies, heart failure,

punctures—not forgetting to put on
  in lipstick several bravely
    inaccurate strawberry smiles.

My father used to teach us,
  "You can influence an opinion
    if it differs from yours in attitude,

but you'll never change an attitude
  if it differs from yours in belief."

I believe you believe

in some really achievable beauty.
    That's what undoes us both
        in the Finchley Road.

You emerge from the underground,
    Englishman in an England
        you'd prefer not to have lost.

Blame me, if you like—American
    from America I'd prefer
        still to love.

"England? You live in England?"
    yells my New York taxi driver.
        "Why don't you live someplace

you can make a few bucks?"
    I want bucks.
        i want you more than bucks,

O England of the old books
    that never was until
        it finds itself in us.

This

isn't making love.
This is feeding off the substance of
what was made when we were made.

This is the body unafraid
of the soul. This is Abelardian glut
in a starved school.

This is negation of adulthood's rule
that talks by rote.
This is travelling out to where

a curved adventure
splashes on planes of sunlight to become
one perfectly remembered room,

white walls, white wings of curtain, window
screened but opened wide
to cricket chirr in a field where no

discovery is new.
This is the always has been. What we do
is home. And this is I and you.

Winter Time

Cobalt water
wrinkled under thin ice.
Last day summer time.

Remembering to turn the clock back.
For loving, a precious hour.
For living, no more time.

In candlelight from their grining
hollowed-out turnips—
Ethiopian children.

Hiroshimas of children,
yet I mourn for the collie with the white neck
killed on the roadway.

Mist raining or rain misting?
Woods like an antique tapestry
the cat's got at.

You dream of betrayal
on a paradisiacal island.
I wake in guilt.

Naming the flowers

for Lionel Elvin

makes no difference to the flowers.
These inside-out parasols,
orb webs on crooked needles,
grey filmy cups in the clockwork
of summer goatsbeard

are to themselves not "seeds",
not "systems of distribution",
never the beards of goats,

but to us they anticipate
bare patches, old age, winter-time.

They tell us to pronounce now
all that we wish to keep.

My fields of recollection
already are yellow with toadflax.
Wheels of sky-blue chicory
purl into purple angelica;
hogweed is taller than my sons.

The path I will follow is

shocking with unfinishable steeples;
"foxglove", I'll say, then "balsam",
"rose bay willow herb", "red campion".

I'll note particularly
the pinched licorice temper of my fingers,
pods of sweet cicely. Scabious
will be last into my grey-blue coma,
reminding me of heaven,
the shell-frail colour of harebells.

In winter time my bare patch
will be heavy with names.
I am only a namer.
Only the names are seeds.

May Swenson

O'Keeffe Retrospective

Into the sacral cavity can fit the skull of a deer,
the vertical pleat in the snout, place of the yoni.
Within the embrasure of antlers that flare, sensitive
tips like fingers defining thighs and hips, inner horns
hold ovary curls of space.

Where a white bead rolls at the fulcrum of widening knees,
black dawn evolves, a circular saw of polished speed;
its bud, like Mercury, mad in its whiz, shines, although
stone jaws of the same delta, opposite, lock agape—
blunt monolithic hinge, stranded, grand, tide gone out.

A common boundary has hip and hill, sky and pelvic basin.
From the upright cleft, shadow-entwirled, early veils
of spectral color—a tender maypole, girlish, shy, unbraids
to rainbow streams slowly separated.

A narrow eye on end, the lily's riper crack of bloom:
stamen stiff, it lengthens, swells, at its ball (walled pupil)
a sticky tear of sap. Shuttlecock (divided muzzle of the dried
deer's face, eyeholes outline the ischium) is, in the flap of
the jack-in-the-pulpit, silken flesh. As windfolds of
the mesa (regal, opulent odalisque) are, saturate orange, sunset.

Cerulean is solid. Clouds are tiles, or floats of ice
a cobalt spa melts. Evaporating, they yet grip their shapes;
if walked on, prove not fluff and steam. These clouds
are hard. Then rock may be pillow, stones vacant spaces.
Look into the hole: it will bulk. Hold the rock: it will empty.

Opposite, the thousand labia of a gray rose puff apart,
like smoke, yet they have a fixed, or nearly fixed, union,
skeletal, innominate, but potent to implode, flush red,
tighten to a first bud-knot, single, sacral.
Not quite closed, the cruciform fissure in the deer's
nose bone, symphysis of the pubis.

Where inbetweens turn visible blues, white objects vanish,
except—see, high at horizon on a vast canvas sky—
one undisciplined tuft, little live cloud, blowing:
fleece, breath of illusion.

View to the North

As you grow older, it gets colder.
You see through things.
I'm looking through the trees,

their torn and thinning leaves,
to where chill blue water
is roughened by wind.

Day by day the scene opens,
enlarges, rips of space
appear where full branches

used to snug the view.
Soon it will be wide, stripped,
entirely unobstructed:

I'll see right through
the twining waves, to
the white horizon, to the place

where the North begins.
Magnificent! I'll be thinking
while my eyeballs freeze.

How to Be Old

It is easy to be young. (Everybody is,
at first.) It is not easy
to be old. It takes time.
Youth is given; age is achieved.
One must work a magic to mix with time
in order to become old.

Youth is given. One must put it away
like a doll in a closet,
take it out and play with it only
on holidays. One must have many dresses
and dress the doll impeccably
(but not to show the doll, to keep it hidden).

It is necessary to adore the doll,
to remember it in the dark on the ordinary
days, and every day congratulate
one's aging face in the mirror.

In time one will be very old.
In time, one's life will be accomplished.
And in time, in time, the doll—
like new, though ancient—may be found.

Bee Bee Tan

Pontianak

When we died,
I finally gave birth.
It was then the villagers called me
Pontianak, roaming vampire.

My baby on my hip,
I ride the wind;
farmwives and children quiver.
When the sky is wrung grey
and heavy clouds hang low,
it is my day to run
through the village by the river.

My baby whines.
We are blood hungry, thirsty.
Leaves whirl in wind,
and long nipah palms clash.

From the throes of birth in death,
I ride a raft bound with rawhides,
my baby by my side
On the river-raft, we spin past glades
like Shaitans released from Hades.
The Kinta River foams white;
tin sludge is carried low;
alluvium clay becomes mud.

My long hair, wind tossed, is my veil;
my shroud, my sail.
Draped in blood,
we eat the land;
my baby lives the way it dies.

Curfew

I smell lavender in trays late nights when I
forget my keys and climb like a burglar
through open windows. The house is black

and soundless with sleeping idiots. I have
walked in dark arts, and warm nights with leaves
yellow like allamandas' poison. Boards have creaked
under my feet as I step over the sill,
dragging clay on leather slippers.
The moonlight presses steep and white
on my back while flower-bells part their lips
whisper in sultry heat and the green salt odor
of sea-flowers' gleaming. Summer lightning
winks over trees stretching beyond my sight
and when I hear mother walking to the bath
I am tempted to shrink into the wall, become
one of ten rose buds in rows of ten by ten.

Susan Tichy

In 1945, on her way to receive the Nobel Prize, Gabriela Mistral passed through her former home, Temuco, Chile, in the dead of night. According to Pablo Neruda, she contrived to do so because she was offended by the townspeople's conviction that she could not have written so movingly of childbirth unless she, herself, had borne a child. The title of this poem is from Gabriela's "Una Piadosa."

The Cry That Kills the Senses: Meditation After a Nightmare

In the casket a corpse of wicker.

Waking, I look over the neighbor's hill
to the pale line of April mountains,
see there, in the dark, a valley of rice and pine.

How far to the burning plain?

On a night train in 1945, Lucila Godoy Alcayaga
passed through Temuco, exhausted
by her sleepless child—a raw, meticulous pain.

They were lifting the lid. They were showing me.

Yet how often, speaking with strangers,
I see them turn their faces, look deeply
into a cavern I can't see.

Light came from a torch or burning tree.

This much I see: in 1985, in the Carcel de Temuco,
a man banged his cup on the door of his cell.
Carlos Gabriel Godoy, aged 23,
died of a sudden difficulty breathing.

They had dragged it out to the mouth of the cave.

So which is the dream—when the body vanishes,
or when it reappears, face-down, face-up,
contorted in the unforgettable yoga?

I was there with it forever—

I was never there, Temuco,
but I know it's hard to breathe
with a man's thumbs on your throat.
Is this what you say is unsayable?

233

—a corpse woven skilfully from thick brown stalks of grass.

Don't you hear? Though it never sleeps, she sings:
in a small hour the train sways
and rocks the mind's precision near the heart.

My husband's hand waking me, I heard a voice. It was mine.

Never mind, Temuco. This was all some other country.
It's only dreaming that's confused me,
the tribal caskets piled so carelessly on each other.

An artifact, that's all.

It was 1945. In a moment of weakness the world
turned to a noncombatant. Even a child, she wrote,
should sooner starve than eat the unjust bread.

Orpheus

from Africa, for Suzanne in Asia

When I first saw him he was standing on wet pebbles
of a road in Fez, and so was I, though he turned,
at once, into a crowd and vanished, utterly,
just as now he vanishes—like vapor
into dry air, like thought into the straining body
of memory, a city unto itself,

with the stink of piss-cured leather, a rattle
of tin and brass embossers, louder with each
turn of the street, narrowing, then flaring,
like the ear's canal, into a yard of sun
falling through leaves of a single tree
on hammers, plates, cauldrons,
and the dull brown clothing of the men,

who stare, then offer glasses vivid
as aquariums with live, sweet mint.
It raises in the mouth a taste of mountain,
as the wall of a mosque, inlaid with pebbles,
lends to the skin a touch of stream, leaf, stone,
with fragile sunrise full of colors only
a corner of the eye can see—all leading not

to vaulted spaces of the sacred court,
but to a spice-shop's sudden lavender and thyme,
to the steep wet cobbles of the next street,
darker, where a dyer's donkey staggers under red—

vanishes, as sun into the darkening skin,
as rain into a river running beneath the streets, beneath
the cracked, infected hooves of an overloaded mule

darkening the gate of a yard like prayer in the mouth of a man
with his forehead pressed to the ground.
Under him, too, it runs, under women selling oranges
spread in their laps, a fountain coming up

where the poor drink and wash their feet
on entering a mosque, they who have no shoes
to remove, whose thirst is visible
from the ancient battlements, a dust languishing
in the wind's arms, falling on the city like a curse
as the wind tires. . . Carefully, now: I see him.

He appears as I climb from the bus, inhale
his first dirty breath. I'm startled
by the rude hands of children
cutting light to pieces, by fear itself hovering
with irridescent wings of a small bird
at my head, so I falter, stunned

by the long fall from dreams, into sprays
of my own language coughed back at me like blood,
surprised that I am visible through the bright
silk wrappings of an unseen face. He appears,
then vanishes, like stick-thin, bloated figures
bobbing at sleep's edge. So, what I follow

over cobbles lost to moss, under arches
holding rooms and families—not to light
glancing on the hills and branches, but deeper
into this oldest city—is a voice, male
and willowy, a voice beginning where the smell
of orange peels and burned meat puts my mind to sleep,
and leading past all knives, all metal-work and singing,
to a street of odors struck up by hooves on stone.

And the voice, now, is water. And the river,
now, is in me. And the great city turns
like a wheel on a sudden quiet. He looks,
but I am not there. He has my face. I have
his gifts—jasmine and black thread. I wait
alone for the cool nerve that equals great desire. . . .

Then will I bend and enter
that souk, of all the souks,
where sits a woman just my size,
faintly bent and sewing in the dark.

Kitty Tsui

Don't Call Me Sir Call Me Strong

i get called sir
all the time.
by women, by men,
waitresses in restaurants,
salesclerks behind counters,
stewards on board planes.

it's the short hair
that sets them off.
or maybe it's because
i stand tall,
have a wide stance,
broad shoulders
and thick forearms.

or perhaps it's
my wristwatch
made for a man.

i get called sir
all the time.
i even get cruised
by men in the castro
out looking for fresh meat.

i suppose it's because
i have small breasts,
big fists,
walk with hands in pockets,
stand tall
with a wide stance,
broad shoulders
and thick forearms,
i'm taken for a man.

it's time to talk back.
hey, don't call me sir
call me strong
call me sassy
call me spirited
call me sure-of-myself
call me competent
call me confident

call me powerful
call me proud.
don't call me sir
call me strong.

call me
woman who walks
with a long stride,
woman with small breasts,
big fists,
hands in pockets,
standing tall
with a wide stance,
broad shoulders,
thick forearms
and wears a man's watch.

don't call me sir
call me strong.
call me shooting star
call me sea
call me wave upon wave
call me womb
call me woman.

a strong woman sighing
a sassy woman loving
a spirited woman working
a sure woman singing
a competent woman rejoicing
a confident woman crying
a powerful woman chanting
a proud woman coming.

a proud woman
coming into herself.

from Red Rock Canyon, Summer 1977

(iv) the vision
trekking back along the high trail
i, still in my bare feet,
stopping at intervals
to pick desert flowers for pressing.

trekking back along the high trail,
the soles of my feet, tender.
i stop n look to the sky.
there is a cloud formation—a dragon!

i stop nita. look to the sky!
there is a cloud formation, a dragon.
at the dragon's mouth the sun is setting.
i sink to my knees, humble.

nita and i on our knees in the sand
staring in wonder at this sight.
the sun is red orange, glowing
at the dragon's mouth.

at the moment of climax,
the sun at the dragon's mouth,
she disintegrates into luminosity.
i fall limp onto the sand.

at the moment of climax
i see a vision superimposed on the sky,
i see my lover's face as she comes in my arms.
i fall limp onto the sand.

chinatown talking story

the gold mountain men said
there were two pairs of eyes
so beautiful
they had the power
to strike you dead,
the eyes of
kwan ying lin
and mao dan so.

kwan ying lin, my grandmother,
and mao dan so
were stars of the
cantonese opera
and women
rare
in a bachelor society.

when my grandmother first came
to gold mountain in 1922
she was interned on angel island
for weeks, a young chinese girl,
prisoner in a strang land.

when mao dan so
first arrived
she came on an entertainer's visa
and made $10,000 a year.

it cost $1.25 to see a show,

a quarter after nine.
pork chop rice was 15¢.

when theater work was slow
or closed down
other work was found:
washing dishes,
waiting tables,
ironing shirts.

in china
families with sons
saved and borrowed
the $3,000
to buy a bright boy
promise in a new land.

in china
girls born into poverty
were killed or sold.
girls born into
prosperity
had their feet bound,
their marriages arranged.

on angel island
paper sons and blood sons
waited
to enter *gum san*
eating peanut butter on crackers
for lunch and
bean sprouts at night.

the china men who passed
the interrogations
were finally set free.
the ones who failed
were denied entry and deported
or died by their own hands.

in 1940, the year
angel island detention center
was closed
a job at macys
paid $27 a week.
only chinese girls
without accents please apply.

my grandfather had four wives
and pursued many women
during his life.
the chinese press loved
to write of his affairs.

my grandmother,
a woman with three daughters,
left her husband

to survive on her own.
she lived with another actress,
a companion and a friend.

the gold mountain men said
mao dan so was as graceful
as a peach blossom in wind.
she has worked since
she was eight.
she is seventy two.
she sits in her apartment
in new york chinatown
playing solitaire.
her hair is thin and white.
her eyes, sunken in hollows,
are fire bright when she speaks.

the gold mountain men said
when kwan ying lin
went on stage
even the electric fans stopped.

today
at the grave
of my grandmother
with fresh spring flowers,
iris, daffodil,

i felt her spirit in the wind.
i heard her voice saying:

born into the
skin of yellow women
we are born
into the armor of warriors.

Mona Van Duyn

Letters from a Father

I

Ulcerated tooth keeps me awake, there is
such pain, would have to go to the hospital to have
it pulled or would bleed to death from the blood thinners,
but can't leave Mother, she falls and forgets her salve
and her tranquilizers, her ankles swell so and her bowels
are so bad, she almost had a stoppage and sometimes
what she passes is green as grass. There are big holes
in my thigh where my leg brace buckles the size of dimes.
My head pounds from the high pressure. It is awful
not to be able to get out, and I fell in the bathroom
and the girl could hardly get me up at all.
Sure thought my back was broken, it will be next time.
Prostate is bad and heart has given out,
feel bloated after supper. Have made my peace
because am just plain done for and have no doubt
that the Lord will come any day with my release.
You say you enjoy your feeder, I don't see why
you want to spend good money on grain for birds
and you say you have a hundred sparrows, I'd buy
poison and get rid of their diseases and turds.

II

We enjoyed your visit, it was nice of you to bring
the feeder but a terrible waste of your money
for that big bag of feed since we won't be living
more than a few weeks longer. We can see
them good from where we sit, big ones and little ones
but you know when I farmed I used to like to hunt
and we had many a good meal from pigeons
and quail and pheasant but these birds won't
be good for nothing and are dirty to have so near
the house. Mother likes the redbirds though.
My bad knee is so sore and I can't hardly hear
and Mother says she is hoarse from yelling but I know
it's too late for a hearing aid. I belch up all the time
and have a sour mouth and of course with my heart
it's no use to go to a doctor. Mother is the same.
Has a crab she thinks is going to turn to a wart.

III

The birds are eating and fighting, Ha! Ha! All shapes

and colors and sizes coming out of our woods
but we don't know what they are. Your Mother hopes
you can send us a kind of book that tells about birds.
There is one the folks called snowbirds, they eat on the ground,
we had the girl sprinkle extra there, but say,
they eat something awful. I sent the girl to town
to buy some more feed, she had to go anyway.

IV
Almost called you on the telephone
but it costs so much to call thought better write.
Say, the funniest thing is happening, one
day we had so many birds and they fight
and get excited at their feed you know
and it's really something to watch and two or three
flew right at us and crashed into our window
and bang, poor little things knocked themselves silly.
They come to after while on the ground and flew away.
And they been doing that. We felt awful
and didn't know what to do but the other day
a lady from our Church drove out to call
and a little bird knocked itself out while she sat
and she brought it in her hands right into the house,
it looked like dead. It had a kind of hat
of feathers sticking up on its head, kind of rose
or pinky color, don't know what it was,
and I petted it and it come to life right there
in her hands and she took it out and it flew. She says
they think the window is the sky on a fair
day, she feeds birds too but hasn't got
so many. She says to hang strips of aluminum foil
in the window so we'll do that. She raved about
our birds. P.S. The book just come in the mail.

V
Say, that book is sure good, I study
in it every day and enjoy our birds.
Some of them I can't identify
for sure, I guess they're females, the Latin words
I just skip over. Bet you'd never guess
the sparrows I've got here, House Sparrows you wrote,
but I have Fox Sparrows, Song Sparrows, Vesper Sparrows,
Pine Woods and Tree and Chipping and White Throat
and White Crowned Sparrows. I have six Cardinals,
three pairs, they come at early morning and night,
the males at the feeder and on the ground the females.
Juncos, maybe 25, they fight
for the ground, that's what they used to call snowbirds. I miss
the Bluebirds since the weather warmed. Their breast
is the color of a good ripe muskmelon. Tufted Titmouse
is sort of blue with a little tiny crest.
And I have Flicker and Red-Bellied and Red-
Headed Woodpeckers, you would die laughing
to see Red-Bellied, he hangs on with his head

flat on the board, his tail braced up under,
wing out. And Dickcissel and Ruby Crowned Ringlet
and Nuthatch stands on his head and Veery on top
the color of a bird dog and Hermit Thrush with spot
on breast, Blue Jay so funny, he will hop
right on the backs of the other birds to get the grain.
We bought some sunflower seeds just for him.
And Purple Finch I bet you never seen,
color of a watermelon, sits on the rim
of the feeder with his streaky wife, and the squirrels,
you know, they are cute too, they sit tall
and eat with their little hands, they eat bucketfuls.
I pulled my own tooth, it didn't bleed at all.

VI
It's sure a surprise how well Mother is doing,
she forgets her laxative but bowels move fine.
Now that windows are open she says our birds sing
all day. The girl took a Book of Knowledge on loan
from the library and I am reading up
on the habits of birds, did you know some males have three
wives, some migrate and some don't. I am going to keep
feeding all spring, maybe summer, you can see
they expect it. Will need thistle seed for Goldfinch and Pine
Siskin next winter. Some folks are going to come see us
from Church, some bird watchers, pretty soon.
They have birds in town but nothing to equal this.

So the world woos its children back for an evening kiss.

Lisa Vice

Houston Street

they huddle over garbage fires
moving from foot to foot
heat passing quickly through their rags
they gulp coffee
gleaned from the pockets of passersby
fresh from showers
where hot water is never a miracle
from homes
where thick rolls of toilet paper
are never luxuries

they never ask me for money
something uncertain
in my newly leathered feet
tells them
something uncertain
in the way I clutch my morning token
tells them
there is a thin line between us

we are not busy people
hurrying to breakfast in steamy cafes
to offices
where coffee perks all day

in the evening
a man in a playboy hat
face down in the gutter
empty bottles
pools of puke
the one legged man
still hustling
to polish windshields

a man on a stoop asks me for a cigarette
I see my brother
in his broken teeth   matted hair
my groceries grow heavy in my arms
he asks me to marry him
the only man who ever dared
I laugh and wink

he knows   I know
how these greasy streets feel

to cold bare feet
we both know
how quickly
the fine line between us melts

To the Waitress at the Hickory Pit

You call me love
hug me as only a stranger can
making me long for my mother
I haven't missed her in years
I don't want tonight's special
take me home with you instead
let me hear the grit on your shoes
scratch the linoleum
show me your dusty china dog collection
change into a chenille housecoat
fry onions and hamburger for s.o.s.*
I'll butter the toast
we can eat together
in front of the blue t.v. glow

*s.o.s.: "shit on a shingle," a dish composed of hamburger and onion
         with milk gravy (the shit) over toast (the shingle).

Cambodia Witness

sun shines in Heng Chor's eyes
curtain of light touches his wife
her lips
molded
in denial her husband will never speak
seven day old son
naked on her lap

if you slip a knife into the brain
through the roof of the mouth
twist the thin blade slowly
chickens die with no pain

i catch her rolling feathers in the dust
cooing under her breath
i tuck her under my arm
carry her to the barn

feathers
dust
twisting knife
tiny eye staring
waiting
sunlight glaring on metal
twisting
sky so blue it hurts
seven day old boy
knows only his mother's touch
drinks blank terror in her milk
swallows his dead brothers
swallows his dead sisters

one hand holds her down
the other twists
sun falls behind the barn
tiny eye
staring
out of kindness
i spread her neck across the stump
a quick clean slice

my fingers clutch the beating wings
the headless dance
pounds through my hands
beak opens and closes
opens
on the sawdust floor

who witnessed Heng Chor's dead
carved into the eyes of his nameless wife
5 sons
3 daughters
8 from his sister-in-law's family
7 from his brother-in-law's family

eggs with no shells
drop
into a bucket of feathers
each yolk smaller
and smaller
long fingers stained with blood
fly on the knife

warm rains wash
bleached skulls
in shallow pits
eyes bound with cloth
hands strapped to a stranger's

rope to wrist
fingers speaking to fingers
darkness
growing darker

Diane Wakoski

I Have Had to Learn to Live with My Face

You see me alone tonight.
My face has betrayed me again,
   the garage mechanic who promises to fix my car
   and never does.

My face
that my friends tell me is so full of character;
my face
I have hated for so many years;
my face
I have made an angry contract to live with
though no one could love it;
my face that I wish you would bruise and batter
and destroy, napalm it, throw acid in it,
so that I might have another
or be rid of it at last.

I drag peacock feathers behind me
to erase the trail of the moon. Those tears
I shed for myself,
sometimes in anger.
There is no pretense in my life. The man who lives with me
must see something beautiful,

like a dark snake coming out of my mouth,
or love the tapestry of my actions, my life/this body, this
face, they have nothing to offer
but angry insistence, their presence.
I hate them,
want my life to be more.
Hate their shadow on even my words.

I sell my soul for good plumbing
and hot water,
           I tell everyone;
and my face is soft,
opal,
a feathering of snow
against the
          cold black leather coat
which is night.
          You,
          night,

my face against the chilly
expanse
of your back.
Learning to live with what you're born with
is the process,
the involvement,
the making of a life.
And I have not learned happily
to live with my face,
that Diane which always looks better on film
than in life.
I sternly accept this plain face,
and hate every moment of that sternness.

I want to laugh at this ridiculous face
of lemon rinds
and vinegar cruets
of unpaved roads
and dusty file cabinets
of the loneliness of Wall Street at night
and the desert of school on a holiday
but I would have to laugh alone in a cold room
Prefer the anger
that at least for a moment gives me a proud profile.

Always, I've envied
the rich
the beautiful
the talented
the go-getters
of the world. I've watched
myself
remain
alone
isolated
a fish that swam through the net
because I was too small
but remained alone
in deep water because the others were caught
taken away
It is so painful for me to think now,
to talk about this; I want to go to sleep and never wake up.
The only warmth I ever feel is wool covers on a bed.
But self-pity could trail us all, drag us around on the bottom of
shoes like squashed snails so that
we might never fight/ and it is anger I want now, fury,
to direct at my face and its author,
to tell it how much I hate what it's done to me,
to contemptuously, sternly, brutally even, make it live with itself,
look at itself every day,
and remind itself
that reality is
learning to live with what you're born with,
noble to have been anything but defeated,

that pride and anger and silence will hold us above beauty,
though we bend down often with so much anguish for
a little beauty,
a word, like the blue night,
  the night of rings covering the floor and glinting
  into the fire, the water, the wet earth, the age of songs,
  guitars, angry busloads of etched tile faces, old gnarled
  tree trunks, anything with the beauty of wood, teak, lemon,
  cherry
I lost my children because I had no money, no husband,
I lost my husband because I was not beautiful,
I lost everything a woman needs, wants,
almost
before I became a woman,
my face shimmering and flat as the moon with
with no features.

I look at pictures of myself as a child.
I looked lumpy, unformed, like a piece of dough,
and it has been my task as a human being
to carve out a mind, carve out a face,
carve out a shape with arms & legs, to put a voice inside,
and to make a person from a presence.
And I don't think I'm unique.
I think a thousand of you, at least, can look at those old photos,
reflect on your life
and see your own sculpture at work.

I have made my face as articulate as I can,
and it turns out to be a peculiar face with too much
bone in the bridge of the nose, small eyes, pale lashes,
thin lips, wide cheeks, a rocky chin,
But it's almost beautiful compared to the sodden mass of dough I
     started out with.

I wonder how we learn to live
with our faces?
They must hide so much pain,
so many deep trenches of blood,
so much that would terrorize and drive others away, if they
could see it. The struggle to control it
articulates the face.
And what about those people
With elegant noses and rich lips?

What do they spend their lives struggling for?

Am I wrong I constantly ask myself
to value the struggle
more than the results?
Or only to accept a beautiful face
if it has been toiled for?

Tonight I move alone in my face;
want to forgive all the men whom I've loved

who've betrayed me.
After all, the great betrayer is that one I carry around each day,
which I sleep with at night. My own face,
angry building I've fought to restore
imbued with arrogance, pride, anger and scorn.
To love this face
would be to love a desert mountain,
a killer, rocky, water hard to find, no trees anywhere/
perhaps I do not expect anyone
to be strange enough to love it;
but you.

Coda: Greed Part 12—
Looking for Beethoven in Las Vegas

The music in my head again,
not lily pad orchestra
or ebony flute,
the opening of yucca bells,
a creamy swish of lips,
the waver of pink and yellow,
Opuntia, cresting flesh,
Ocotilla flame, piercing air,
clear sounds of the flowers.

My car pointed West,
the trunk full of diamonds,
and Mother rattler coiled there.
We are travelling to Southern California
to the Pacific,
where surfers
and angel-boy-men worship sun,
where the Osprey Sisters search for their piano,
where the moon bathes,
and the foggy canyons wrap their shot silk
around old bodies.

Still, there is a destination
which must be accomplished first,
a search for Beethoven in the
casinos of Las Vegas. Why
search for him
in this gaudy city
where ham and eggs are served
24 hours a day?
where dawn is dewy
but freshness is only in the mind,
the carpets permeated with smoke,

the upholstery stale with gin and perfume.
But I heard his sounds here once.
Never, in the subways of my city,
New York;
never, in the pounding of the Atlantic on steeply sloping beaches
when the sun nudged my tips
and wound round the sprocket of desire;
never, in the adobe missions
and terra cotta roofs
of empty California life;
never, in the thick wheat-filled, asparagus-tipped, peach-laden,
                                        corn-spiked
summers or
ice-clotted winters
of Michigan;
not even on the cobblestone streets of Hydra, waking, caught
                                    like a cormorant,
with the ring around my throat, and looking
deep into the squid-clear Mediterranean;
or in the green-grey olive trees on the rocky hills of Majorca
where a man in pain was moaning in his cold kitchen.

I listened for his music
as I walked through Beethoven's park
in the Gringinerstrasse,
Vienna spring, where I did hear
La Traviata and fancied as I wandered through the Schönbrunn,
hearing Mozart's piano music accompanying my steps,
but I did not hear Beethoven's music
even elusively,
not once,
till I walked into the MGM Grand
and heard the thunk thunk thunk
of silver dollars
rattling into the slot machine tubs;
there it was,
thunk, thunk, thunk,
Beethoven's Sixth Symphony;
there it was,
a string quartet;
there it was,
the Apassionata Sonata;
Fidelio;
a Bagatelle;
thunk, thunk, thunk, thunk, thunk, symphonies
in George's coin,
the silver dollar from which
he had his Camp Cup made;
thunk, thunk, thunk,
this history of America,
that is,
the U.S.A.
played in a new symphonic thrust

when those silver dollars
clatter out of the machines in Las Vegas,
in the American desert,
the sound beyond The Strum,
the sound created by Beethoven, Americanized and
wandering in the desert,
looking for someone to love.

So, my journey has taken me there,
aching elbows, old acorns of the East
rattling in my empty joints,
making another music,
the one of aging and bone-crack death,
of sleeping alone and
tending the garden,
of looking out through the lacy curtains of one's life,
seeing the desert as the only future,
no strawberries on the lips now,
or moist canteloupe.

I hold in my hand a cardboard cup
as big as a child's head.
It is filled with silver dollars
I have received in exchange
for paper money. They weigh
down my hand
as the past has never weighed me down.
It is the future
which now is so heavy,
as heavy as a 6,000 B.T.U. air conditioner,
or a small refrigerator,
or 24″ pot with soil, containing a mountain ash tree.
As heavy as a mortgage and a house
your lover
doesn't want to live in.
It is the prospect of sleeping alone
every night, and the books
no one
will ever read.

It is the pain of your husband
swallowing sleeping pills in an anguish you can do nothing about,
or worse, your lover turning away from you
to other lovers,
or saying to you he would leave
you,
rather than hurt you/ you've
been hurt so much, but you
wondering why he doesn't think
leaving you
would be a source of pain.

When I dream of this city,
Las Vegas, I am
bare-armed,

long-haired,
scented with lilies of the valley
wrapped in raw silk,
shod in glass or gold,
looking nothing like
I ever looked in youth or life,
playing Chemin de Fer,
escorted by a man who wins at the dice tables, and I hear
Beethoven's symphonies
because they are big and melodic and my
life is big and melodic.

But when I am in this mythic city,
I am a small plump woman,
swathed in tent-like clothes,
sitting in the Keno parlour, reading
Henry James and playing 90¢ games.
I listen to the
thundering next to me in the bank
of slot machines, the tinkle,
the ringing,
and the thunk, thunk, thunk, thunk, thunk
of silver dollars
clanging into the metal pans.
It is Beethoven's music
but he is not here.
None of the men I love
are ever where
I look for them.
My map,
the Moon's map:
The Mare of Isolation,
The Mare of Remote Shadows,
The Mare of Longing,
No geography which would ever yield
what I have
searched for.

Driving West,
old, enlightened,
I still cannot fold up those
maps of lost goldmines,
abandoned trunksfull of diamonds,
of new countries and other planets.
I still listen for Beethoven at the ocean,
and George Washington in the desert.
But my own voice fades
into the landscape,
perhaps is only heard through
the unspoken language of desert flowers.

Marilyn Nelson Waniek

Mama's Promise

I have no answer to the blank inequity
of a four-year-old dying of cancer.
I saw her on t.v. and wept
with my mouth full of meatloaf.

I constantly flash on disaster now;
red lights shout *Warning. Danger.*
everywhere I look.
I buckle him in, but what if a car
with a grille like a sharkbite
roared up out of the road?
I feed him square meals
but what if the fist of his heart
should simply fall open?
I carried him safely
as long as I could,
but now he's a runaway
on the dangerous highway.
Warning. Danger.
I've started to pray.

But the dangerous highway
curves through blue evenings
when I hold his yielding hand
and snip his miniscule nails
with my vicious-looking scissors.
I carry him around
like an egg in a spoon,
and I remember a porcelain fawn,
a best friend's trust,
my broken faith in myself.
It's not my grace that keeps me erect
as the sidewalk clatters downhill
under my rollerskate wheels.

Sometimes I lie awake
troubled by this thought:
It's not so simple to give a child birth;
you also have to give it death,
the jealous fairy's christening gift.

I've always pictured my own death
as a closed door,

255

a black room,
a breathless leap from the mountain top
with time to throw out my arms, lift my head,
and see, in the instant my heart stops,
a whole galaxy of blue.
I imagined I'd forget,
in the cessation of feeling,
while the guilt of my lifetime floated away
like a nylon nightgown,
and that I'd fall into clean, fresh forgiveness.

Ah, but the death I've given away
is more mine than the one I've kept:
from my hand the poisoned apple,
from my bow the mistletoe dart.

Then I think of Mama,
her bountiful breasts.
When I was a child, I really swear,
Mama's kisses could heal.
I remember her promise,
and whisper it over my sweet son's sleep:

> When you float to the bottom, child,
> like a mote down a sunbeam,
>   you'll see me from a trillion miles away:
>   my eyes looking up to you,
>   my arms outstretched for you like night.

Dinosaur Spring

A violet wash is streaked across the clouds.
Triceratops, Brachiosaurus, Trachodon
browse the high greenery, heave through
the dissipating mists.
They are as vacant as we are:
They don't see how mountains are growing,
how flowers change spring by spring,
how feathers form.

Last night I walked among the dinosaurs,
hardly taller than a claw.
I touched their feet with my fingertips,
my tongue numb with wonder.

At seven this morning two mallards
and a pair of Canada geese
preened themselves in the light of the pond.
Awake on a morning like this one,
jays screeching from treetop to fencepost,

I have to strain to imagine
how people wake up
in San Salvador, in Cape Town, in Beirut.
The background roar grows louder,
a neighbor screams for her child.

Just now I took my baby out of his crib
and teetered on the edge of the vortex.
I saw millions of hands imploring,
mouths open, eyes his.
I fell into a universe of black, starry water,
and through that into monstrous love
that wants to make the world right.

I can comfort my son:
The ghost in the closet, the foot-eating fish
on the floor can be washed away
with a hug and a tumbler of milk.
But the faceless face? The nuclear pinata
over our heads? The bone finger pointing?

Through the window I see the sky
that hung over the dinosaurs.
The flight of a grackle catches my eye
and pulls it down toward the moving water.
I can't see the larger motion, leaves
moldering into new soil.
If I lay on my back in the yard,
I'd feel how we're hanging on
to this planet, attached even to her
by the sheer luck of gravity.

I have to shake my head, I've grown so solemn.
It's my turn to vacuum the house.
In the din, I go back to my dream:
Holding my son by the hand,
I walk again among the dinosaurs.
In my breast my heart pours and pours
so that it terrifies me, pours and pours out
its fathomless love, like the salt mill
at the bottom of the sea.

Roberta Hill Whiteman

Acknowledgement

> I fight so they will recognize me and treat me like a human being.
> Rigoberto Machu, ***Journey to the Depths***

Listen, for the Lord
of the Near and Close comes
to make you see
in steam rising from coffee,
smoke from bodies burning in Panzos.
Sometime he'll have you taste
in your chocolate bars
that bitterness children carry
when they dare not bury
their bludgeoned mothers.

On the backs of owls,
Ixquic, Woman's Blood, flew
out of smoldering hells,
carrying within her twins
who restored freedom
to those sunlit mountains.
Sometime she'll have you smell
in the red and fragrant flowers
hearts of boy soldiers,
hanging in trees.

Where is the Mirror
That Makes All Things Shine?
The night wind's my Lord.
He cleans the bodies flung in ravines,
and comforts aching women,
standing before their fragile fires.
His breath's a spiral
wide as this galaxy
where nothing is obscured.

Obsidian Butterfly will force you to see
how children sleep in a cardboard box
year after tremulous year. In the span
of their hands, onions, gruel, and
a dangerous abyss
for the people of this sun.
In clouds and mist, their suffering moves.

Something comes to wake you.

Something comes without faltering.
Can you feel it in the twilight?
In your fruits and in your cheeses,
In your signatures?
The gods and goddesses are talking together,
scanning dumpsters and smog,
nuclear playgrounds. They soothe
cholera-stricken geese, and the broken
feet of coyotes.

In their diminishing forests
they meet, counting the heartbeats
it will take to make
each face sublime.
Will you acknowledge the love
and faith of our restless earth,
or will you claim the suffering's
too far south while your mouth
samples and measures, calls everything
tangible?

Through darkness, through night
our suffering moves,
a slow quake in the chest, a sigh.
No food and the body will eat itself.
Some of you bluster and do not believe
we have cut the heart of the sky.

You give gasoline to the lords
of your death,
spoon out the sugar,
ignoring its tears.

Fogbound

Last night
the moon let her uncarded wool
spill over these houses
and hills

Now
beyond my door
the woods recede into a labyrinth
of latent waves
while the pomp pomp of dew
dripping from eaves
measures the music
of her passage

From his fencepost

a storm-colored rooster
cocks his head
listening
for the distant tread of the sun

but the moon fashioned even stones
into sponges
When it doesn't   come
he crows

All the unnamed beings
beyond this crossroad
answer
who are you that the sun
should come first
to your flat eyes

Above this maze of edges
flies a woodpecker
whose red head sways like a lantern
in the sea's spindrift

I lift my life
to the moon this autumn morning
toast with my breath
all she's left me
I dance down the road in her honor
dance back   singing
rapt in the wet wool
of her buried world

where nothing is discerned
or decided very long
where bushes and branches multiply
into meandering herds
into egrets rising in frothy silence

where every flicker
of lifting mist
bears witness to another encounter

Through such a world
I'd walk to Guatemala
carrying the moon's cochineal
still living in my cape
I'd wear them
draped like crimson kisses
through those turbulent mountains

if only
I knew by now
you had crossed the river
where thick fibers have scrubbed off
summer's green
There oaks gleam as copper and umber
as wood voles slumbering
underneath

if only

that spider hadn't captured
the world's four winds
in the roof's overhang
In her spangled web
they strain
while she works the whorl and spindle
of herself
in her web the polar lights
the muddy fragrance of March lilacs
the secret echoes
of swallows perched in hedgerows
after a summer rain

while you head west
my alien
into a subdued morning

In Mosa's Time

for Jackie Whitman

They found him looking north
dreaming how we'd leave those shallow days
the wash, the rooms of mending,
to roam with him and praise
his far snow-clouded plain.

You called him Mosa, Mandan for coyote,
and loved his wary eye, his wandering mood.
He knew, he knew the storms of Spring
bring changes. Those eager winds elude
us as we watch through a rusted screen,

a stark other self, rooted in dirt, hoping
to flower amid syllables of rain.
Bud trembles into leaf
and what comes to us again
is a muffled dying and a certain obscure birth.

Snow was leaving cloud prints on the hills
that morning we drove to Rapid. A hawk
hung low in the heavy sky, and radials
slapped the wet road. We talked
of men and coyotes, of dolphins

that once swam this inland sea.
How tough, how rare it is to love through time.
Jackie, your words helped me endure

261

those nights I muttered at the grime
in rooms too red to love or bleed in.

Mosa proved his strength was running.
He'd leap a fence and go for miles,
a gait quick as spoondrift,
a silver shadow answering the wiles
of a changing wind.

As he played with a collie
in and out the woods one sweet warm dawn,
my soul's fragment, faithful
to its ache, said I had hung on
and loved the dreams more than the man.

In their game, both wild and tame
taught me we must lose to keep alive.
In Mosa's time, blue as a sudden sadness,
the grackles cheered and more arrived
with a returning world.

My heart soared until dreaming
didn't matter. The buds turned green
and hurt our eyes and Mosa was shot dead.
Yet under summer skies, he runs unseen.
The smallest wind that moves, knows this
and loves him still.

Nellie Wong

Have Head, Have Tail

The hurt is red. It is a sore with a big, big eye.
Tears grow on me like new hair. Why is pain a giant
when I am asked: Do you plan to get married again
and do you plan to have children?

Child, child, what do you know? I could strike you dead,
I could ring the bells. But Ma would shriek:
Do not raise your hands! She is young
and you must teach.
Even if I blurt out my 48 years,
my sister's and my faces are whited out.
In dream. In the living room.

The right to free speech.
Jeanne Kirkpatrick walks out when students hiss.
She has the right to free speech
any time
anywhere
because she defends
U.S. imperialism.
But Merle Woo?
Merle Woo gets fired
from the classroom.
She speaks about democracy.
For students, staff and faculty. Against censorship.
For a Third World College. Against cultural genocide.
For lesbians and gays. Against heterosexism.
For the possibility of all our voices,
in all languages, singing out.

I own no podium. Only the fierceness of fingers
that scratch and type.
The sky is red. As is love, desire, passion.
I stand accused: You speak nothing
but political rhetoric.

Me, grandiloquent? Me, insincere?
Ai yah, cheong hay poa boomerangs!
She flies on a broom, dusts well-worn shelves.

They are unbrave, these Stalinists who won't debate.
Asian American women
as Trotskyists

as revolutionary feminists
as internationalists?
Tsk, tsk! Such audacity, such muscular yellow legs!

Fish cannot fly, but we women can write.
If I reveal my perversion for T.V.'s "The Love Boat,"
they will capture
my unique personality.
If I reveal that I love women,
they will justify
their impoverishment.

When a pillow is a companion, something must be
wrong.
The independent Asian woman just cannot be.
She's as unfathomable as an ancient tung tree.
Going public, going strong.
Writing at midnight in the nude.
What matter is newsprint which dwells
on femininity?
We want to know you, not your politics,
you, Bolshevik machine, you!

If I criticize the revolutionary family,
they would explode.
If I stress socialism in one country,
they would smile, invite me, perhaps,
to tea.
By golly, I'd be delirious, plenty ho hum.

Find new words or dig up the old.
Sound less positive, kiss ass, blow old smoke.
Capitulate to the pressures, be accepted
to fit the sexist, racist, anti-leadership mode.
Whoa! My little Chinese girl, my soul, my soul.

Fight with your night, hear what Bah Bah said:
Yew how, mo mee.
Have head, no tail.
Ai yah, thlom meen nui, gay haw gow ah hei ngom neh?
Ai yah, little girl-child, how can I teach you right?
If you wash the dishes, the sink will shine.
If you do your homework, courage will find you.

Yew how, mo mee.
Have head, no tail.
Bah Bah, you never explained.
Aphorisms were never a game.
I turn it around: Yew how, yew mee.
Have head, have tail.
I touch my own body. Militant. Cantonese.

Yew how, yew mee. Yew seen too.
Have head, have tail, have body too.
Bah Bah, I hear you now, I fight back.

How plump and juicy your white-cut chicken, your bock teet gai.
How constant this, my revolutionary life.

Eat, Eat!

*in memory of my sister Leslie Jow who
died of lung cancer on January 16, 1985*

Ah Ma Ma, Poppa, Leslie
You are all gathered here
Please, sit down, sit down!
I am cooking the rice now.
Drink something first.
Poppa, I'm giving you the ng gah pei whiskey.
Ma Ma, you like just a teeny bit of wine?
Leslie, my younger sister,
you still drink peony tea?
Good! Good!
In my house I have everything.
Get up from your chairs.
Look at these beautiful roses.
Also, I have birds-of-paradise in the garden.
Ummmmm. Also, chrysanthemums, of course.
This Chinese evergreen
is really sturdy, so strong.
Oh, sit down, sit down.
The rice is ready.
I poached this whole chicken myself.
It's really smooth.
You didn't know that I could cook?
This Chinese broccoli is very fresh.
I just went to Chinatown after work to buy it.
I still remember
ah Ma Ma, Poppa, Leslie
you all like to play mah jongg.
Great!
Once we've eaten our meal,
we will start the game.
O.K.?
I wish
everyone will be lucky
everyone wins lots of money
everyone wins full-fan hands
everyone prospers!
Ah, Bill and Joyce
have a beautiful son
His Chinese name is Gee Oong Leng
His American name is Sam

Just like your name, Poppa.
Sam's so animated, knows how to talk
this and that, this and that.
Where are you working, Daddy?
Where's Auntie Les?
Where's my green dinosaur?
We all just love him.
Sit down, sit down.
Come, eat the rice, drink.
Start the meal, start the meal.
Eat, eat!

Evan Zimroth

Separations

Even the small separations
the necessary ones
such as night, or going to work
remind me inevitably
of the others:
a family
lined up
for deportation
exchanging
one swift, indelible
glance as grandmother
is directed to one room
granddaughter
to another, or
Chekhov's Iona
whose son has died, and no one will listen.

Planting Children: 1939

Oh quick, garner the children.
Stash them in baskets, egg crates,
dresser drawers, anywhere;
kiss their thin necks in the hollow
where the blood pulses,
kiss their warm ears. The train already
is raising dust,
the lists are drawn up, the cows
no longer look up from pasture.
It is the iron hinge, the parting.
Now, quick, shove the babies underground
like spuds: let them root there
for forty years, let them
come up story-tellers, all eyes.

Front Porch: A Drama Critic Warns of Clichés

1
When the curtain opens
on a front porch, says the critic,
I walk out, meaning,
I suppose, those ubiquitous
rocking-chairs, an old grand-
ma or pa, the usual cataclysm
of ho-hum raw emotion,
plenitude of gnats, fireflies, and
wisteria at dusk.
Let me not omit
from this banned semiology
of porches, my own front porch
on the Maryland corner
of First and Anson, almost blotted out
by a scrim of rhododendrons
fanged with pink blooms.
This front porch is where

the featureless intruder
stands in my nightmare
peering through windows, searching
for me like a magnet. Where
I lay in a chaise-lounge one hot day
in '55, and Jesse
Something-or-other,
fearless, faceless,
squashed his blond face
against mine and kissed me
full on the mouth, full
of the blond smell of the intruder
and I bolted up, alien, compromised,
having suddenly conceived.

2
Even worse, the critic continues,
someone's mother always has cancer. It's true,
my mother does have cancer,
it's a cliché, a convention, you can hardly
blame her. Probably
I have cancer too, almost certainly;
perhaps it has already leaked down,
down to my two daughters, killing
each other so innocently there on the porch.

Perhaps the clear scrim of blood
is already transformed, the understudies
already warmed up
and taking over. Perhaps in my play
my children will be orphans, almost certainly
I will be an orphan, a tree will fall
on my car, the plane will crash, the gun

will go off, we will lose everything, we will
have to emigrate, we will be jammed
into boxcars, there will be no water, someone
with insignias will meet us, another pogrom
is waiting in the wings. Surely
this is my front porch for life.

Notes on the poets

Katharyn Machan Aal is the Director of the Feminist Women's Writing Workshops, a summer conference based in Ithaca, New York, where she also coordinates a literary arts organization, the Ithaca Community Poets. Her poems have appeared in numerous magazines and anthologies in the United States and she has given more than a hundred public readings of her work. Of her twelve published collections of poems, the most recent is *From Redwing* (Tamarack Editions, 1987).

Ai has published three volumes of poetry, *Sin, Killing Floor* and *Cruelty*, and has won many prizes including a Guggenheim and the Lamont Poetry Prize. She lives and writes in Cambridge, Mass.

Ellen Bass has published several volumes of poetry, the most recent being *Our Stunning Harvest* (New Society Publishers). She is co-editor of *I Never Told Anyone: Writings by Women Survivors of Child Sexual Abuse* and a new book, tentatively titled *The Courage to Heal: A Guide for Survivors of Child Sexual Abuse* (Harper & Row, January 1988). She lives in Santa Cruz, California with her partner, Janet Bryer, and her daughter, Sara. She travels nationally facilitating writing workshops and groups for survivors.

Beth Brant is 45, a North American Indian (Bay of Quinte Mohawk) a lesbian mother of three and a grandmother. She has been writing since she turned 40. She is the editor of *A Gathering of Spirit: Art and Writing by North American Indian Women*, the first anthology of its kind (Sinister Wisdom Books, 1983). She is also the author of *Mohawk Trail* (Firebrand Books, 1985), a collection of poetry and prose. She lives in Detroit with her companion of eleven years, Denise, and one of her daughters.

Barbara Brinson Curiel (formerly Barbara Brinson-Pineda) was born in 1956 in San Francisco, California. An instructor in Creative Writing at the University of California, Santa Cruz, she is a founding member of the Centro Chicano de Escritores, a support organization for Chicano/Latino writers. Her publications include two chapbooks *Nocturno* (Fuego de Aztlan Publications, 1978) and *Vocabulary of the Dead* (Nomad Press, 1985).

Mary Pierce Brosmer was raised in Crestline, Ohio. She graduated from Ohio Dominican College in 1970 and received her MA in English from Xavier University in 1983. Mary lives in Cincinnati with her son, Colin, and teaches English at Milford High School in Milford, Ohio.

Lorna Dee Cervantes was born in San Francisco and raised in San Jose, California. She is active in Chicano community affairs, a member of the Chicana Theatre Group and organizer for the Centro Cultural de la Gente. In 1976 she founded MANGO publications, a small press that publishes a literary magazine and books of poetry. Her own book of poetry, *Emplumada,* was published in 1981 by the University of Pittsburgh Press.

Amy Clampitt was born and brought up in rural Iowa. She graduated from Grinnel College and has since lived mainly in New York City, earning a living in and around book publishing. She began publishing poems in magazines in 1978. Her first full-length collection, *The Kingfisher*, was published by Knopf in the US in 1983, and by Faber & Faber in the UK in 1984. *What the Light Was Like* followed (Knopf, 1985; Faber & Faber, 1986). Her latest collection, *Archaic Figure,* also published Knopf and Faber & Faber, appeared in 1987. She is currently Visiting Writer at Amherst College.

Michelle Cliff is a Jamaican-born writer. Her latest book, a novel entitled *No Telephone to Heaven*, was published in July 1987 by E.P. Dutton. Her most recent collection of poetry and prose, from which these poems were selected, is *The Land of Look Behind*, published in 1985 by Firebrand Books. She is a recipient of a National Endowment for the Arts fellowship in creative writing and a Massachusetts Artists Foundation grant in fiction. She lives in Santa Cruz, California.

Lucille Clifton's works include *Good Times, Good News About the Earth, An Ordinary Woman, Generations: A Memoir, Two-headed Woman, Sonora Beautiful*, and many children's books. She lives in California.

Jane Cooper is the author of *The Weather of Six Mornings* and *Maps and Windows*, both published in the USA by Macmillan, and of *Scaffolding: New and Selected Poems*, published in the UK by Anvil Press Poetry. *Scaffolding* also includes her feminist essay "Nothing Has Been Used in the Manufacture of This Poetry That Could Have Been Used in the Manufacture of Bread." Her first book received the Lamont Award of the Academy of American Poets, and *Scaffolding* was recently given the first Maurice English Poetry Award, for a book by an American poet over 50. She has also been co-recipient of the Shelley Award of the Poetry Society of America, and has had fellowships from the Guggenheim Foundation, the Ingram Merrill Foundation, and the National Endowment for the Arts. She lives in New York City, and has taught at Sarah Lawrence College, the University of Iowa, and the Columbia University School of the Arts.

Jayne Cortez was born in Arizona, grew up in California and is currently living in New York City. Her poetry has been published in many journals, magazines and anthologies including *Confirmation, Powers of Desire, New Black Voices, Giant Talk, Free Spirits, Presence Africaine, Mundus Artium* and the *Unesco Courier*. She is the author of six books of poetry and three recordings. Her most recent book is *Coagulations: New and Selected Poems* and her most recent recording, *There It Is*. She has lectured and read her poetry alone and with music throughout the United States, West Africa, Latin American and the Caribbean.

Thulani Davis is a poet and journalist. She is the author of *Playing the Changes* (Wesleyan University Press), and *All the Renegade Ghosts Rise* (Anemone Press). She has written extensively for the *Village Voice*, where she is a staff writer, as well as for *Mother Jones, Essence* and *The Nation*. Her poetry has been published in numerous anthologies and periodicals. In 1984 and 1985 she was the recipient of NEA and SPDF grants for a radio documentary on black composers, *Fanfare for the Warriors*, which aired on over 250 stations nationwide. She was co-producer and script writer for the documentary and was awarded the First Place Prize in radio from the National Association of Black Journalists in 1986. She recently completed the script for a radio opera by Henry Threadgill which will air on National Public Radio this year. She wrote the libretto for the widely acclaimed opera *X: The Life and Times of Malcolm X* by Anthony Davis, which had its world première at the New York City Opera in 1986.

Angela de Hoyos is a San Antonio poet and visual-artist whose published works include four books of poetry, the latest of which is *Woman, Woman* (Arte Público Press, University of Houston, Texas). Some of her poems have been translated into Portuguese, French, Spanish and German. Her book *Selected Poems (Selecciones,* in Spanish translation by Mireya Robles) was first published in Mexico by Universidad Veracruzana, 1976. Her poetry is the subject of a book-length critical study, *Angela de Hoyos: A Critical Look,* researched and written by Luis Arturo Ramos during an extended visiting position at the University of Mexico in San Antonio. Her work is analyzed as well in the book by Marcela Aguilar-Henson, *The Multifaceted Poetic World of Angela de Hoyos,* recently published by Relámpago Books Press, Austin, Texas. Actively involved in the arts, she serves on the City of San Antonio's Arts and Cultural Advisory Committee and has been appointed to the Martin Luther King, Jr. Memorial City-County Commission 1987. She is co-editor of *Huehuetitlan Journal* and editor of Manda Publications, San Antonio, Texas.

Toi Derricotte has published two books of poems: *The Empress of the Death House* (1978) and *Natural Birth* (1983). Her poems have been published widely in magazines and anthologies including work in *The Iowa Review, Northwest Review, Pequod, Ironwood, 13th Moon* and *Beloit Poetry Journal.* Her poems are included in the third edition of *An Introduction to Poetry,* edited by Louis Simpson. She was a recipient of a National Endowment for the Arts Fellowship in Poetry in 1985. She also received a fellowship from the New Jersey State Council on the Arts, and was a MacDowell Fellow in 1983. She received the Lucille Medwick Memorial Award from the Poetry Society of America in 1985. She has been guest poet at Dartmouth, Barnard, the Library of Congress, the Poetry Center of San Francisco, and more than one hundred universities, libraries and museums throughout the United States.

Diane di Prima was born in New York City. She has been important as a poet and as an editor for the last thirty years. Her books include *Loba, Loba II, Loba As Eve,* and *Selected Poems.* She has lived for some years in California.

Rita Dove was born in Akron, Ohio in 1952 and educated at Miami University (Ohio), the University of Iowa, and the Universität Tübingen. Her books of poetry include *The Yellow House on the Corner* (1980), *Museum* (1983) and *Thomas and Beulah* (1986), all with Carnegie-Mellon University Press. *Fifth Sunday,* a collection of short stories, was published in 1985. A recipient of the Academy of American Poet's 1986 Peter I.B. Lavan Younger Poets Award (chosen by Robert Penn Warren), Rita Dove also has to her credit Fulbright-Hays, National Endowment for the Arts and Guggenheim Fellowships. She teaches at Arizona State University in Tempe, Arizona.

Carolyn Forché was born in Detroit in 1950. Her first book of poems, *Gathering the Tribes,* received the Yale Series of Younger Poets Award for 1975 and was published in 1976 by Yale University Press. Between 1978 and 1980 she lived and worked as a writer and human rights activist in El Salvador. Her second book, *The Country Between Us,* was chosen as the Lamont Selection of the Academy of American Poets, and published in 1981 by Harper & Row. A volume of translations of the poetry of Claribel Alegria, *Flowers From the Volcano,* appeared from the University of Pittsburgh Press in 1982. In 1983 she wrote the text for *El Salvador: The Work of Thirty Photographers,* published by Writers & Readers Cooperative in the UK. She has published articles in *The American Poetry Review, Esquire, Ms., The Nation, The Progressive, Mother Jones* and *Granta*

(England). *The Country Between Us* has appeared in German and Swedish editions, and was a Swedish Book of the Month selection. She has held fellowships from the John Simon Guggenheim Foundation and the National Endowment for the Arts. During the winter of 1983/84, she contributed to the program "All Things Considered" on National Public Radio from Beirut, Lebanon. In 1984, she received a second National Endowment for the Arts fellowship. She lives in Paris.

Celia Gilbert is the author of *Bonfire* (Alice James Books) and *Queen of Darkness* (Viking). She is the winner of a Discovery Award, a Pushcart Prize IX for her poem "Lot's Wife," and an Emily Dickinson Award, given by the Poetry Society of America. She has worked as an editor, teacher, and freelance journalist. She lives in Cambridge, Massachusetts with her husband and has two children.

Melinda Goodman is a lesbian poet living in Brooklyn, New York.

Considered one of America's foremost poets and one of its most provocative voices, **Judy Grahn** lived her first nine years in Chicago, Illinois and the following nine in southern New Mexico. She received her formal education from a number of schools, and has a BA in Women's Studies from San Francisco State University. She has made herself at home on the coast of California since 1968. In 1970 she co-founded the first all-women's press which published, printed and distributed a variety of new women's voices, including her own *Edward the Dyke, The Common Woman Poems* and *A Woman Is Talking to Death*. St. Martin's Press has published a collection of her poetry through 1977, *The Work of a Common Woman* (reprinted by Crossing Press). Grahn has also edited two volumes of women's short stories, and has taught creative writing workshops for several years at the Women's Writing Center at Cazenovia, New York and the Women's Writing Workshop at Oneida, New York and at Ithaca College, Ithaca, New York. She has also taught courses at Stanford University and New College of California. She currently teaches women's writing, poetry, literature and gay and lesbian studies classes in the Bay Area. Her most recent books are *The Queen of Wands* (Crossing Press) and a major nonfiction work, *Another Mother Tongue: Gay Words, Gay Worlds* (Beacon); also *The Highest Apple: Sappho and the Lesbian Poetic Tradition* (Spinsters Ink). She is currently working on a verse play, *The Queen of Swords*, for Beacon Press, and a novel.

Susan Griffin is a poet and writer author of *Woman and Nature, Pornography and Silence* and the Emmy-Award-winning play *Voices*. She is presently at work on a book on nuclear war, *The First and the Last: A Woman Thinks about War* to be published by Doubleday & Co. Her second major collection of poems, *Unremembered Country*, was published by Copper Canyon Press, in 1987. She lives and teaches privately in Berkeley, California.

Marilyn Hacker lives in New York and Paris. Her latest book, *Love, Death, and the Changing of the Seasons*, a novel in sonnets from which the selection in this anthology was excerpted, was published in New York in 1986 by Arbor House and in London in 1987 by Onlywomen Press.

Born and raised in the Philippines, **Jessica Tarahata Hagedorn** is the author of *Dangerous Music* and the award-winning, *Pet Food and Tropical Apparitions*, both published by Momo's Press. Her poems, prose, and plays have been anthologized and produced widely.

Joy Harjo was born in Tulsa, Oklahoma in 1951, and is of the Creek Tribe. She has published three books of poetry, including her most recent, *She Had Some Horses* (Thunder's Mouth Press). She is an assistant professor at the University of Colorado, Boulder, is on the Board of Directors for the Native American Public Broadcasting Consortium, and the Poetry Editor for *High Plains Literary Review*. She also plays tenor saxophone in a big band in Denver.

Linda Hogan is a Chichascuo Indian writer. She is the author of several books of poetry and a collection of short stories. Her latest book, *Seeing Through the Sun*, received an American Book Award from the Before Columbus Foundation. She teaches in American Studies and American Indian Studies at the University of Minnesota, and works as a volunteer in wildlife rehabilitation.

June Jordan is currently Professor of English at S.U.N.Y. at Stony Brook, as well as director of the Poetry Center there. Winner of numerous awards, and recipient of many honors throughout her career, she has published a total of sixteen books. Among the most recent are *Living Room*, (Thunder's Mouth Press, 1985), and *On Call*, (South End Press, 1985), new political essays. The full-length musical drama, *Bang Bang Über Alles*, for which she wrote the lyrics and the libretto, music by Adrienne B. Torf, was presented in its World Première Production at Seven Stages, Theatre, Atlanta, Georgia, in 1986.

Faye Kicknosway's new and selected *All These Voices* was published by Coffeehouse Press in December 1986. She and her daughter live in Honolulu, Hawaii, where she teaches at the University of Hawaii.

Carolyn Kizer won the Pulitzer Prize in 1985 for *Yin*. A long-time feminist, her book *Mermaids in the Basement: Poems for Women* was published in 1984. Her newest book, *The Nearness of You*, was published in 1987.

Irena Klepfisz was a founder and for five years editor of *Conditions* magazine. She is the author of *Keeper of Accounts* (Sinister Wisdom Books) and *Different Enclosures: Poetry and Prose of Irena Klepfisz* (Onlywomen Press). Most recently, she co-edited *The Tribe of Dina: A Jewish Women's Anthology* (Sinister Wisdom Books). She has taught English, women's studies, Yiddish and poetry and fiction writing. An activist in the lesbian/feminist movement, she has given workshops on Jewish identity, anti-Semitism, homophobia and autobiography.

Maxine Kumin is the author of eight collections of poems, the most recent of which, *The Long Approach* (Viking/Penguin), was published in 1985-86. She won the Pulitzer Prize in 1973 for her poems in *Up Country*, an Academy of American Poets Fellowship in 1985, and the Levinson Award from *Poetry Magazine* in 1986. She and her husband live on a farm in New Hampshire, where they raise horses. A collection of her country essays, *In Deep*, was published by Viking in 1987.

Since 1924 **Meridel LeSueur** has been publishing her poetry, fiction and articles. After receiving the kind of attention her work deserved in the first half of her career, she was deemed unfashionable and was neglected for some years. In the last ten years there has been a strong resurgence of interest in her powerful and sonorous work. Her books include *Salute to Spring*, *Rites of Ancient Ripening* and *Harvest: Collected Stories*.

Denise Levertov grew up in England but now lives in the United States. She has published several books of poetry, including her *Selected Poems* and *Oblique Prayers* (both published by Bloodaxe Books), and two of prose. She is represented in *The Bloodaxe Book of Women Poets* edited by Jeni Couzyn.

Lyn Lifshin is an internationally known poet and editor. More than seventy of her books and chapbooks have been published, and she has edited a series of books of women's writing: *Tangled Vines* from Beacon Press (1978), *Ariadne's Thread* from Harper & Row (1982), and a book of women's memoirs.

Audre Lorde is the author of nine volumes of poetry; her most recent volume *Our Dead Behind Us* was published by Norton in the USA and in the UK by Sheba Feminist Publishers in 1987.

Cynthia Macdonald has published four collections of poems, most recently *Alternate Means of Transport* (Knopf). Before becoming a poet she was an opera singer. Born and raised in New York City, she now lives in Houston where she teaches at the University of Houston. Her grants and awards include a Guggenheim Fellowship, National Endowment for the Arts grants, and an award from the National Academy and Institute of Arts in recognition of her achievement in poetry. She has two children.

Colleen J. McElroy is a professor of English at the University of Washington. She is the author of six books of poetry, among them *Queen of the Ebony Isles*, which won the American Book Award in 1984. She has also published a textbook and a collection of short fiction.

Mary Mackey was born and raised in Indianapolis, Indiana, and is related through her father's family to Mark Twain. In 1966 she graduated *magna cum laude* in English from Harvard and in 1970 received her Ph.D. in Comparative Literature from the University of Michigan. In 1976 she became one of the five founders of the Feminist Writers' Guild. At present she is a professor of English and Writer in Residence at California State University, Sacramento, where she teaches creative writing and film. Her published works include three volumes of poetry (*Split Ends, One Night Stand* and *Skin Deep*), a novella, *Immersion*, and three novels (*McCarthy's List*, Doubleday, 1979, *The Last Warrior Queen*, Putnam, 1983, and *A Grand Passion*, Simon & Schuster, 1986). Her latest collection of poetry is *The Dear Dance of Eros* (Fjord Press, 1987).

Elizabeth McKim's books of poetry include *Burning Through* (Wampeter Press), *Family Salt* (Wampeter Press) and *Body India* (Yellow Moon Press). She has published widely in many magazines and journals including *Ploughshares, Sojourner, Epoch* and *Poetry*. A poet who works from the oral tradition of sound, chant and story, she directs poetry workshops for people of all ages throughout the US and abroad. She is a member of the Graduate Faculty of the Arts Institute for Expressive Therapies and Creative Arts in Learning of Lesley College, and she co-authored a book about her teaching entitled *Beyond Words—Writing Poems With Children*.

Donna Masini was born in Brooklyn and now lives on Manhattan's Lower East Side. She is a 1986 recipient of the New York State Foundation for the Arts grant and an American Academy of Poets Award. She has been published in *Conditions, Thirteenth Moon* and *Slow Motion*, and has taught at Hunter College and New York University.

Sharon Olds's books are *The Gold Cell* (Knopf, 1987), *The Dead and The Living* (Knopf, 1984), and *Satan Says* (University of Pittsburgh Press, 1980). A limited edition of her work will be published soon by John Harvey of Slow Dancer Press in England.

Brenda Marie Osbey attended Dillard University, Université Paul Valery at Montpellier, France, and the University of Kentucky at Lexington. A native of New Orleans, she has taught French and English at Dillard University, and was Curator and Researcher at the Louisiana

Division of the New Orleans Public Library, specializing in Louisiana Black and Creole History and French and Creole translations. Her poems have appeared in *Obsidian, Essence Magazine, Callaloo, Tendril Magazine, Southern Exposure*, and *The Southern Review*. She is the recipient of the American Academy of Poets Loring-Williams Prize, and was a recipient of the 1984 AWP (Associated Writing Programs) Fifteenth Anniversary Poetry Competition Award for the poem "Portrait." Named the Bernadine Scherman Fellow of the MacDowell Colony for 1984, she was a Fellow of the Mary Ingraham Bunting Institute at Harvard-Radcliffe for 1985–86. She is the author of *Ceremony for Minneconjoux* (Callalloo Poetry Series, 1983), now in its second printing.

Alicia Ostriker is a poet-critic whose work has appeared in *Poetry, The New Yorker, The Hudson Review, American Poetry Review, The Nation, Ms., Feminist Studies, Women's Studies, Signs, Partisan Review, The New York Times Book Review, Parnassus*, and other magazines. She is the author of six books of poetry, most recently *The Mother/Child Papers* (Momentum Press, 1980, reprinted Beacon Press, 1986) and *The Imaginary Lover* (Pittsburgh University Press, 1986). As a critic, she has written widely on American women's poetry. A collection of her essays, *Writing Like a Woman*, was published in the University of Michigan Press series of Poets on Poetry in 1983. *Stealing the Language: The Emergence of Women's Poetry in America* (Beacon Press) appeared in 1986. Recipient of a 1984 Guggenheim Fellowship, a National Endowment for the Arts award for poetry and a Rockefeller fellowship for humanities research, she is author of *Vision and Verse in William Blake* and editor of Blake's *Complete Poems* (Penguin). Alicia Ostriker is a Professor of English at Rutgers University, and lives with her family in Princeton, New Jersey.

Linda Pastan's sixth book of poetry, *A Fraction of Darkness*, published by Norton in 1985, received the Maurice English Award. She is on the staff of the Bread Loaf Writer's Conference.

Marge Piercy is the author of ten volumes of poetry: *Breaking Camp, Hard Loving, 4-Telling, To Be of Use, Living in the Open, The Twelve-Spoked Wheel Flashing, The Moon Is Always Female, Circles on the Water, Stone, Paper, Knife*, and, most recently, *My Mother's Body*. She has also published nine novels: *Going Down Fast, Dance the Eagle to Sleep, Small Changes, Woman on the Edge of Time, The High Cost of Living, Vida, Braided Lives, Fly Away Home*, and, in 1987, *Gone to Soldiers*. The University of Michigan's Press published a volume of her essays, reviews and interviews as part of their Poets on Poetry series, entitled *Parti-Colored Blocks for a Quilt*. Marge Piercy has also co-authored a play, *The Last White Class*, with Ira Wood. She lives in Wellfleet, Massachusetts with Ira Wood. Her work has been translated into twelve languages.

Born in New York City in 1936 and having spent her youth on the New Mexican desert, **Margaret Randall** left this country in her early twenties. For the next twenty-three years, until her return in January of 1984, she lived in Mexico, Cuba and Nicaragua. She worked as a midwife, translated Latin American poetry and prose and became involved in the women's movement. Her travels also took her to Vietnam, Peru, and Chile where she listened to women's stories and wrote about their lives, and she lectured and shared her poetry and that of others. An internationally acclaimed author of more than forty books, Margaret was also the co-founder and editor of the bilingual literary quarterly *El Corno Emplumado* (*The Plumed Horn*), a bridge between cultures in the decade of the 1960s. A poet, photographer, oral historian, activist and teacher, much of her work over the past twenty years has centered on women and people's culture. She currently teaches in the

Women's Studies Program and American Studies Department at the University of New Mexico (Albuquerque), and reads and lectures throughout the country.

Adrienne Rich was born in Baltimore, Maryland in 1929. She graduated from Radcliife College in 1951 and studied briefly at Oxford in 1952–53. In the 1950s she married and had three sons. Her first book of poems received the Yale Younger Poets Award in 1951; she has published eleven books of poetry and three of prose: *Of Woman Born: Motherhood as Experienced and Institution, On Lies, Secrets and Silence*, and *Bread, Blood and Poetry* (all Norton). She was active in the 1960s in the civil rights and anti-war movements, and since 1970 has worked in the women's liberation movement. Between 1980 and 1984 she was co-editor, with Michelle Cliff, of the lesbian/feminist journal *Sinister Wisdom*. The poems in this anthology are included in her most recent book of poems. *Your Native Land, Your Life* (Norton, 1986).

Ruthann Robson was born in 1956, and lives in Florida with a small child and a large dog. Her work includes fiction, poetry, essays, criticism and "scholarship" and has been published in many periodicals and anthologies, including feminist journals such as *Conditions, Room of One's Own, Trivia, Kalliope, IKON* and *Labyris*, and anthologies such as *Speaking for Ourselves: Southern Women's Voices* (Pantheon, 1985). In addition to being a writer, she is an attorney, teacher, unwed mother, and relentless feminist.

Wendy Rose was born in 1948 in Oakland, California. She lives and teaches American Indian studies in Fresno, California. She shares a household with Arthur Murata, a magician who teaches judo, a large cat named Sap, assorted reptiles and amphibians, and a group of rats headed by a patriarch named Bubonic. Her most recent book of poetry is *The Halfbreed Chronicles and other Poems* (West End Press, 1985).

Sonia Sanchez is the author of twelve books including *Homecoming, We A BaddDDD People, Love Poems, I've Been A Woman: New and Selected Poems, A Sound Investment and Other Stories* and, most recently, *Homegirls and Handgrenades*. In addition to being a contributing editor to *Black Scholar* and the *Journal of African Studies*, she has edited two anthologies: *We Be Word Sorcerers: 25 Stories by Black Americans* and *360° of Blackness Coming At You*. A recipient of an NEA for 1978–79 and the Lucretia Mott Award for 1984, she is a winner of a 1985 American Book Award for her book *Homegirls and Handgrenades*. Sonia Sanchez has lectured at over 500 universities and colleges in the United States and has traveled extensively, reading her poetry in Cuba, England, the West Indies, the People's Republic of China, Norway, and Australia. She is Professor of English at Temple University.

May Sarton, poet, novelist, keeper of journals and memoirist, has published forty-two books, but has always believed that if you are a poet, poetry comes first. She was born in 1912, and came to the United States in 1916 with her parents, refugees of World War I. She now lives in York, Maine, by the sea.

Kathleen Spivack is the author of prose and poetry. Her most recent books are *The Beds We Lie In* (New and Selected Poems, Scarecrow Press, 1986), a Pulitzer Prize nominee, and a book of short stories, *The Honeymoon* (Graywolf Press, 1986). She has held a National Endowment for the Arts grant, two Massachusetts Artists Foundation Fellowships, Merit Aid grants, a Radcliffe (Bunting) grant, and was a Discovery Winner. She lives in Watertown, Massachusetts with her two sons.

Anne Stevenson was born in England and brought up in Ann Arbor where she was three times a Hopwood winner at the University of Michigan. She has lived in Great Britain for most of her mature life and is the author of seven volumes of poetry. Oxford University Press published her *Selected Poems* in March 1987, which is available in paperback in the U.S.

In Other Words, New Poems by **May Swenson**, was published by Alfred A. Knopf in 1987. This is Swenson's tenth collection. She has also translated a book of selected poems by the Swedish poet Tomas Tranströmer, and her own work was recently published in Italy, translated by Gabriella Morisco. May Swenson grew up in Utah, but has lived in the New York area since 1950.

Bee Bee Tan is presently doing research in Malaysia on nonya or Straits-born Malaysian Chinese women. Presently she works as a freelance food columnist for the local papers. She is a graduate of the English Creative Writing Department of the University of Washington, Seattle, and ranks Colleen J. McElroy as one of her major influences.

Susan Tichy's first book, *The Hands in Exile*, was published by Random House in 1983 as a National Poetry Series selection. Her poems have appeared most recently in *Northwest Review, Southern Poetry Review, Five Fingers Review*, and *California Quarterly*. Others are forthcoming in an anthology, *Colorado*.

Kitty Tsui was born in the City of Nine Dragons in the Year of the Dragon. She grew up in Hong Kong and England and immigrated to Gold Mountain in 1968. She was one of the founding members of *Unbound Feet*, and is presently working with *Unbound Feet Three*, a collective of three Chinese American women writers who perform original material. A professional freelancer, she is the oral historian for a Chinese theater history project, and the author of *The Words of a Woman Who Breathes Fire*.

Mona Van Duyn has published six books of poetry. She has won the Bolhingen Prize and the National Book Award, is a member of the Academy-Institute of Arts and Letters and is a Chancellor of the Academy of American Poets.

Lisa Vice was raised in Cicero, Indiana. She has been a homeless teenager, an unwed mother, a farmer, a secretary, a birth control counsellor, a sales girl in a subway card shop, a mason's tender, a blueberry raker and a silversmith's apprentice. She just graduated from college and teaches remedial English in New York City.

Diane Wakoski was born in Whittier, California in 1937 and educated at the University of California, Berkeley. She has published sixteen collections of poems and many slim volumes of poetry. She is the Writer in Residence at Michigan State University. She continues to believe that everything that is important about her is contained in her poems.

Marilyn Nelson Waniek is the author of two collections of poetry: *For the Body* (Louisiana State University Press, 1978) and *Mama's Promises* (Louisiana State University Press, 1986). She teaches at the University of Connecticut (Storrs).

Roberta Hill Whiteman, a member of the Oneida Tribe of Wisconsin, published her first collection, *Star Quilt* (Holy Cow! Press) in 1985. She is an Assistant Professor of English at the University of Wisconsin—Eau Claire. Her work has appeared in many magazines and anthologies since the early 1970s.

Born and raised in Oakland, California, **Nellie Wong** is a long-time clerical worker, a member of Radical Women, the Freedom Socialist Party, and the clericals union, AFSCME 3218, at the University of California, San Francisco. She has published two books of poetry, *Dreams in Harrison Railroad Park* (Kelsey St. Press) and *The Death of Long Steam Lady* (West End Press). Her work has appeared in numerous anthologies and journals including *This Bridge Called My Back*, *Echoes from Gold Mountain*, *13th Moon*, *Conditions*, *Real Fiction*, *Working Classics*, *Bridge: Asian American Perspectives*, *Ikon 4*, *Breaking Silence: An Anthology of Contemporary Asian American Poets*, *The Women Writers Calendar 1984*, and *Artists Against Apartheid*. She is co-featured with Mitsuye Yamada in the documentary film *Mitsuye and Nellie, Asian American Poets*, produced by Allie Light and Irving Saraf.

Evan Zimroth is the author of *Giselle Considers Her Future* (Ohio State University Press, 1978), and a second collection of poetry, *Front Porch*. She won a Fellowship in Poetry from the New York Foundation for the Arts, 1985–86, and has recent work in *Poetry*, *The Little Magazine*, and *The Atlantic*. She teaches at Queens College, City University of New York.

PANDORA

Pandora Press is a feminist press, an imprint of Routledge & Kegan Paul. Our list is varied—we publish new fiction, reprint fiction, history, biography & autobiography, social issues, humour—written by women and celebrating the lives and achievements of women the world over. For further information about Pandora Press books, please write to the Mailing List Dept. at Pandora Press, 11 New Fetter Lane, London EC4P 4EE or in the USA at 35 West 35th Street, New York, NY 10001-2291. Some Pandora titles you will enjoy:

Stone, Paper, Knife by Marge Piercy centres on the loss of an old love and the beginning of a new love, a woman's politics and identity rooted in the land and expressed in poems of grieving, of loving, and of deep and fundamental concern with the sources of life and the survival of our species and our world.

"It is a poetry remarkably free of artifice for artifice's sake, free of posturing of any sort. It is direct, powerful and accessible without being unsubtle."
Erica Jong, *The New York Times Book Review*

"They are rough, direct, hairy, political, tremendously energetic, visionary, vulnerable and real."
Margaret Atwood

"Marge Piercy writes highly charged poems about death, sex, love and a wide range of other social experiences. Her perceptive eye can be tough and precise."
Time

£3.95 net   ISBN 0–86358–022–X

PANDORA

My Mother's Body, Marge Piercy's tenth book of poetry, takes its title from one of her strongest and most moving poems, the climax of a powerful sequence of poems to her mother. Rooted in an honest, harrowing, but finally ecstatic confrontation of the mother-daughter relationship in all its complexity and intimacy, it is at the same time an affirmation of continuity and identification.

Readers of Marge Piercy's previous collections will not be surprised to encounter her mixture of the personal and the political, her love of animals and the landscape. There are poems about doing housework, about accidents, about dreaming, about bag ladies, about luggage, about children's fears of nuclear holocaust; about tomcats, insects in the rafters, the influence of a name, appleblossoms and blackberries, pollution and some of the ways women objectify one another.

My Mother's Body is one of Marge Piercy's most powerful and balanced collections.

Price: £4.95   ISBN 0–86358–062–9